Jesus for ever

facts and faith
by
John Wijngaards

CTS

First published 1987 by the
Incorporated Catholic Truth Society
38-40 Eccleston Square, London SW1V 1PD

©1987, John Wijngaards

ISBN 0 85183 706 9 AC

Calligraphy: Jackie Clackson
Cover illustration: The Holy Face, Georges Rouault,
courtesy of the Collezione d'Arte Religiosa Moderna.

Printed by Staples Printers Rochester Limited, Love Lane, Rochester, Kent.

CONTENTS

CONTENTS

1

the search for a believable faith

I am one of those odd people who believe in Jesus Christ. Believing in a Creator is not that difficult. Faced with the mystery and wonder of existence it is easy enough to believe we are dependent on an Ultimate Reality. Accepting a moral code, seeking some form of meaningful meditation, calling oneself an 'intelligent agnostic', is commonplace. It ranks you among sensible people. But believing that God revealed himself in Jesus is quite a different story. It makes you less than entirely respectable, somehow.

Take my friend Lydia who was baptised I don't dare to guess how long ago, but who has not been near a church for at least thirty years. Curled up on her sofa with a glass of sherry in her hand she taunts my credulity. 'If you'd been born on the Ivory Coast, you'd have made an excellent voodoo priest!' For her, Jesus Christ was just another religious preacher like so many others. 'If there is a God then, whoever he is,' (she shrugs her shoulders), 'he would never do such a silly thing as "becoming flesh". The idea is naive and ludicrous!'

Then there is my good friend Paddy, who is even more of a problem. Paddy takes every word of scripture literally. Having had a singular conversion experience in recent years he sees miracles in everything that happens. When I impatiently look at my watch on an Underground platform, he closes his eyes, mumbles some words and then reassures me: 'We will catch that train from Euston. The Lord who could still the storm and walk on the water can also control British Rail.' It is good to know at any time that at least someone can control British Rail; but to make Jesus Christ no more than a super-manager responsible for smoothing out every-day life for his followers seems to be more than far fetched!

Philip is different again. He is a minister, chaplain to a polytechnic. As we drive home from an ecumenical gathering, he offers me his own view on Christ. 'I'm not interested in the historical Jesus. I know he wasn't God. He never rose from the tomb. He never expected to be made a saviour, poor chap! What matters for me is what God is telling me through the inspired Scriptures here and now.' Speeding up to catch the tail end of the orange light he continues: 'What difference does it make what happened in Palestine two thousand years ago? God saves me *now,* in Christ.' In my mind's eye I see his faith as a film reeling off continuously in the present, with no memory of what went before, no clear expectation of what is to come. It does not satisfy me.

Where do I stand, I wonder? Lydia laughs at me because she thinks I believe incredible things. Paddy shakes his head at my lack of faith. Philip prays that I may receive enlightenment one day. Is it so odd, I ask myself, for me to *combine* Lydia's critical attitude, Paddy's readiness to believe and Philip's determination to live in the 'here and now'? Was this what Paul meant when he wrote: 'Jews demand miraculous evidence and Greeks want to be intelligent. As for me, I proclaim the crucified Christ, a message that upsets the Jews and is considered nonsense by the others. Yet Christ is both God's power and God's wisdom. What seems to be God's nonsense is wiser than human intelligence, and what seems to be God's weakness is stronger than human strength' (1 Cor 1:22-25).

When I reflect on my own Christian conviction I see how true Paul's words are. Given my own scepticism about miracles and divine interventions I would never have accepted the incredible story of God becoming human in Jesus had I not, at the same time, *felt* the healing and liberating experience of his power. Love is not communicated by words. As small children we learn to believe our mother's love because she fondles us, plays with us, feeds us and cares for us. Unless the salvation which Jesus brings touches the core of our being, it will mean nothing to us.

This does not mean that believing is no more than an emotional surrender. Quite the contrary. Belief rests on an insight, on a profound intellectual grasp of a dimension of truth that had earlier escaped us. If we believe that Jesus is God's revelation *in history,* then such an insight cannot come about without *historical* evidence.

I am going to try a very difficult undertaking. I will attempt to explain to people like Lydia, Paddy and Philip why my belief in Jesus makes sense to me. This, I know, will pose a challenge. It is not the scientific or academic aspects that frighten me. What I am concerned about is how I can also share my *living faith.* I want to show that a modern, scientific approach and personal commitment to Christ can happily complement each other. It will make this book both an objective report and a subjective witness. I hope it will succeed in explaining what makes me tick as a twentieth-century believer: a Christian who is both critical and convinced.

My first step will be to reflect on story and history; and on truth which transcends both. Is Jesus Christ a historical person in the ordinary sense of the word? Read about this in the next chapter . . . .

2

the face of the MASTER

The story of Jesus Christ is surely the most influential narrative mankind has ever known. Translated into virtually all languages, fragments of this story are read out and preached upon in millions of Christian services every Sunday. Think of the beatitudes; the miracle of Jesus' changing water into wine at Cana; his parables of the good Samaritan, the prodigal son, the unforgiving servant; Jesus' passion, death and resurrection. How many people have been inspired by such texts throughout the centuries! And they inspire us still. The staying power of Jesus' story is truly remarkable.

But what about the historical value of these texts? Can they be relied upon? Do they report events that actually happened? Were they not written down nineteen hundred years ago when the science of history had not yet been invented? How do we know whether what they narrate about Jesus Christ is true? Could they perhaps be beautiful *legends,* moving no doubt, useful as material for reflection, but legends nonetheless, without a solid historical foundation? These are important questions. For our belief in Jesus as the Son of God is based on the reliability of that story.

The answer to these questions is that the story of Jesus

is not just history but *salvation history*. By this I mean that while the story is firmly rooted in history, its scope goes beyond ordinary history. It transcends history. Its meaning surpasses the specific events narrated. It is a kind of history that contains values and truths greater than itself.

We cannot understand the gospels or accept their credibility without an appreciation of this. The best way to show what I mean by the 'transcendent quality' of the gospels is by way of one clear example. I suggest that for this we turn to a reflection on Jesus' face. What did Jesus look like? What do we know about his face?

A face no one could forget

It is common belief that we can tell much about a person's character from his or her face. 'Honest labour bears a lovely face.' 'A good face is a letter of recommendation.' 'After a certain age every man is responsible for his face.'[1] Love or anger, sincerity or habitual deceit, cowardice or courage leave their marks on a person's face. Being the exceptional person he was, Jesus must have had an exceptional face. Many must have looked at his face attentively, his disciples with admiration, the sick with hope, sinners with trust, the scribes perhaps with contempt and suspicion. We may well imagine that no one who had met Jesus could forget his face.

The incredible fact, however, is that we do not know what Jesus looked like. No drawing or painting of his face has been preserved. No one of the generation that knew him has left us a description of it. Did Jesus wear a beard or not? Was he dark skinned or light? Did his mouth, his nose, his eyes have distinctive features? We will never know. 'We do not know his appearance,' St Augustine lamented in the fourth century. An incredible omission, it would seem, on the part of those entrusted with the task of handing down knowledge about the Master.

The earliest image of Christ we possess is a wall painting in Dura-Europos dating from about AD 232. It represents Christ in the stylised form of a teacher, dressed in classical robes, sandals on his feet, a scroll in his hand. At about the same time figures of Christ as the good shepherd appear in the catacombs. After that the number of images rapidly increases and soon proliferates beyond counting. Christ's face is painted and sculptured. It finds expression in mosaics and frescoes. It is immortalised on the reliefs of tomb stones and in stained glass windows. It is the focal point on crucifixes and passion scenes. It reappears in a thousand forms on illustrated manuscripts. In fact, Christians were so anxious to know Christ's facial expression that a host of legends arose, such as the story of Veronica's cloth on which Christ was said to have impressed his features during the way of the cross. Sometimes fake relics were fabricated. When the Crusaders found a holy shroud at Antioch its bearded image, like that of the Turin Shroud, influenced representations of Christ throughout Christendom.[2] Later generations of Christians, it would seem, *had* to imagine and visualise the face of Christ. Why the reticence in the first century?

Perhaps people at the time did not know how to preserve copies of faces or were not interested in them? Archaeology, however, teaches us differently. It is true that the Jews were reluctant to make images of living people since it appeared to go counter to the first of the Ten Commandments. But among the hellenised nations of the Roman Empire the art of making portraits was both well known and widely practised. After all, already in the first few decades, the bulk of the first generation of Christians had become hellenistic. To them the making of portraits was commonplace.

Statues and paintings were made of kings, magistrates, members of senatorial families and even wealthy businessmen. It has come to light that the Emperor Augustus, who ruled from about 30 BC to AD 14, deliberately promoted an 'image' of himself that portrayed him as a youthful, vigorous and virtuous leader. From a description left of him by the historian Suetonius we know that the Emperor actually possessed some ugly features. 'He had clear bright eyes, but only a few teeth which were small and dirty. His hair was yellowish and slightly curly. His eyebrows met and his nose jutted out and then turned inwards. He was neither dark nor fair.' Augustus, however, saw to it that an idealised image of himself was designed, modelled on the classical spear-carrier of Polykleitos. Copies of the model were despatched to all corners of the Roman Empire so that statues of him could be set up everywhere. To date at least 250 of such statues have been found throughout present-day Libya, Egypt, Turkey, Greece, Italy, France, West Germany and Spain. From Roman coins that have been found in the same countries we know that the official, idealised image of the Emperor was engraved on coins struck in at least 136 cities.

In other words: at the time of Christ both the art of preserving accurate representations of people's faces and of 'image building' through visual representations was well established.[3] Could the same skill not have been used to preserve for us the likeness of Christ's face?

But, you might object, to the early Christians Christ's face was not important. This was not the case. The face of Christ was recognised as one of the places where revelation broke through. Christ was the exact image of

I see his blood upon the rose
and in the stars the glory of his eyes,
his body gleams amid eternal snows,
his tears fall from the skies.

I see his face in every flower
the thunder and the singing of the birds
are but his voice —
and carven by his power,
rocks are his written words.

All pathways by his feet are
his strong heart stirs   worn,
the ever-beating sea,
his crown of thorns is twined with every thorn,
his cross is every tree.

JOSEPH MARY PLUNKETT 1887-1916

God (2 Cor 4:4). He reflected the brightness of God's glory. He was the exact likeness of God's own being (Heb 1:3). God's glory shone in the face of Christ (2 Cor 4:6). In John's Gospel Christ can say: 'Who sees me sees the Father' (Jn 14:9). The early Christians were well aware that the humanity of Christ, and this applied particularly to his face, mediated God's revelation. What would have been more natural than to record once and for all the exact features of his face?

How then to explain the omission? Indifference? Incompetence? Hardly. The only explanation that does justice to the facts is the *transcendent* interest of the early evangelists and preachers. They *were* interested in the face of Christ but they considered the *salvific role* of his face more important than the distinctive features themselves, such as the shape of his mouth, the size of his nose, the colour of his skin, and so on. This may seem paradoxical to us, even strange. Yet we have to come to terms with it if we want to understand the nature of the gospel witness. Yes, as a carpenter from a particular family in Nazareth, Jesus' face had its distinctive traits. The apostles may have described these to their early converts. Yet these distinctive traits were not considered important enough to be recorded as part of the official teaching, since it was the shining through of the Father, not the human characteristics, that counted. It reveals a mentality different from that of journalists. It may horrify photographers and historians. The fact is that the early Christians were so convinced of the *transcendent* meaning of Jesus' face that the external details of a description no longer mattered.

What a pity! we might think. Wrong. For it is precisely by its lack of narrow specification that Christ's face has been able to exercise its central role in Christian spirituality. We only need to study the enormous variety of treatment given to portraits of Christ through the centuries to recognise this. The shepherd boy of Roman times, the majestic Byzantine Christ, the Man of Sorrows of the Middle Ages, the triumphant perfect man of the Renaissance, and the searching Christ of modern times all illustrate how the fact of the Incarnation can be an endless source of new inspiration. We realise then that every generation can create its own image of Christ; not thereby denying the features of the man of Nazareth, but doing justice to yet another aspect of his *transcendent* significance.[4]

> That one Face, far from vanish, rather grows,
> or decomposes but to recompose,
> becomes my universe that feels and knows.
>
> Robert Browning

If the story of Jesus focusses our attention on realities that go beyond secular events, what then is the role of the science of history in its regard? This is, indeed, a question we need to discuss.

3

the science of history and truth that transcends

I remember once having a discussion about all these things with a friend of mine. 'The decisive factor for me,' he told me, 'is what professional historians say about it. Do *they* accept the gospels as trustworthy evidence? Would *they* use them as valid sources for Jesus' life?'

He voiced a common demand. Many people, both inside and outside the Church, would be inclined to agree. They believe that the truth of the Jesus story should be determined by the objective scrutiny of scientific history. They would give historians the final word.

It is an assumption that needs to be challenged. The modern sciences can help us in the study of the gospels, as I will show in this book, but they can never establish the *truth* of the story of Jesus. The reason is that history and faith operate on different planes, although sometimes they overlap. We know this from everyday life. Suppose I am impressed by one of John Constable's paintings. It makes me discover the charm of a picturesque village scene. What can scientists do? An analyst may determine the age of the canvas. An art historian may authenticate it as a piece by the master. An antique dealer will fix its price. But the *message* of what the artist is saying can be verified only by a *viewer* like myself. For the artist addresses me as a viewer, not as an analyst, historian or antique dealer. In the same way, the truth of the gospels can be verified only by the believers whom they address, not by historians.

Let us take the episode narrated in John 5:1-18. Jesus, we are told, visited the pool of Bethesda in Jerusalem. It was a place reputed to effect miraculous cures. Many sick people used to lie around there waiting for such a cure, which they believed took place 'whenever the water stirred'. They thought it was an angel touching the water. Jesus passed by, took pity on a man who had been paralysed for thirty-eight years and healed him. This led to a confrontation with the scribes, for that day happened to be a sabbath. According to them, practising medicine broke the sabbath rest. They accused Jesus of not bothering about God's law.

Jesus replied, 'My Father is always working and I too must work.' The meaning of this reply is clear. 'God doesn't stop being a Creator on the sabbath. For instance, wounds continue to heal whether it is sabbath or not. I too continue doing my work of healing.'

This angered the scribes even more, for they rightly understood the implication. 'He calls God his own father,' they said to each other. 'He makes himself equal to God.'

The scribes miss the point. By curing the paralytic Jesus has just proved that he can heal as his Father does. Instead of accusing Jesus, the scribes should turn to him to be cured of their own spiritual paralysis!

Suppose we are asking the question: Is what the writer of this gospel tells us true or not? To answer this we first have to establish clearly what he *is* telling us. For clarity's sake we might distinguish three statements:

1. Jesus cured a paralytic at the pool of Bethesda.
2. Jesus claimed equality with God.
3. If we believe in Jesus he can cure us too.

The third statement is the most important one. For the whole purpose of the gospel is to make us accept Jesus as our saviour. John tells us that he wrote his gospel 'that you may believe that Jesus is the Son of God and that through your faith in him you may live' (Jn 20:31). Put in a nutshell, the story teaches us that Jesus can heal us spiritually as much as he cured the paralytic physically. But this is a *religious* statement. It appeals to our faith. It asks for commitment. Obviously, the truth or falsehood of the statement will depend on the validity or invalidity of the *religious* claims made. The statement demands a *religious* answer. So although considerations of historical truth are not irrelevant (if, for example, it could be shown that Jesus had never existed at all, never cured anyone, never made any messianic claims, the beliefs of his followers would be shown to be groundless), ultimately the truth of the statement has to be assessed by religious norms and falls outside the scope of the secular historian.

It may be worth going into this matter even more deeply. Strange as it may seem, 'truth' varies in nature according to the kind of knowledge we are dealing with, as many modern studies have shown. That 'two and two make four' is true in mathematics in the sense that the two sides of the equation are equal. That 'Hitler lost World War II' is true in history as an event that actually took place. In literature, a work of fiction can still be said to be 'true' in the sense that it reflects real life. Scientific 'truth' is sometimes defined as the body of observations and theories which have received the assent of the community of scientific workers at a given time.

Such a shift in the meaning of truth is not a quibble about words; it makes a real difference. This also applies to religious truth.

Religion is neither mathematics, nor history, nor literature, nor science. It does not concern things, but people. It concerns people's relationship to God, a Reality not covered by secular disciplines. Religious truth is therefore conveyed by 'convictional language' and relates to questions of existential meaning, of commitment to the ultimate.[5] The truth of the proclamation 'Jesus can heal us as he healed the paralytic' falls outside the scope of doctors, newspaper reporters and historians. It is transcendental truth, the truth conveyed in the story of salvation.

You may think that I am overstating my case. Surely doctors, reporters and historians can make some valid observations that have a bearing on the statement? Indeed they can. But such observations will always fall short of assessing the religious claim itself.

Observable facts and recorded events

A historian's services are useful all the same. We could ask him or her, for instance, 'Are there within this religious story facts that can be historically verified?' It is a limited task we seek, like requesting a dentist to give advice on a scene in a film script or a vet to examine a horse's leg before a race; yet it is helpful.

Turning to our story the historian may fasten his attention on a specific detail. 'Near the Sheep Gate in Jerusalem there is a pool with five porches. In Aramaic it is called Bethesda' (Jn 5:2). Can we prove the existence of such a pool at the time of Christ?

Some critics have denied that the reference is accurate. 'John's Gospel was written three-quarters of a century after Christ's death,' they contend. 'It was composed in Asia Minor far away from Jerusalem, fifty years after Jerusalem had been destroyed. How can we credit it with any historical precision?' One confidently asserted that the evangelist invented the details of the location for the sake of symbolism. The 'Sheep Gate' reminds us that Christ is the Good Shepherd, he said. The name Bethesda means 'house of mercy'. The five porticoes refer to the five books of Moses on which the Jews rely for salvation.[6] Others maintained that John had transferred to Jerusalem the story of a healing which from the synoptic tradition (Mk 2:1-12) we know to have taken place in Capernaum.[7]

In fact, historical research has vindicated John. In 1914 excavations in the area north-west of the Temple uncovered a huge reservoir trapezoidal in form, about seventy yards wide and a hundred yards long, divided into two pools by a partition in the middle. The reservoir had been hewn from the rock in Maccabean times, and during the reign of Herod the Great colonnades had been built on the four sides and on the dam in the middle. This explains the 'five porticoes' mentioned by John.

Another archaeological find forty years later brought confirmation regarding the name Bethesda. In one of the 'Dead Sea Scrolls', the so-called 'Copper Scroll', discovered in the third cave at Qumran, we read: 'Look at *Bethesdathayin,* near the partition, there where you enter its smaller pool.' *Bethesdathayin* means 'the house of the two springs'.[8] The pilgrim from Bordeaux who left us the earliest written record of a European Christian visiting the Holy Land (AD 333) tells us the pool could still be seen in his time. 'Inside the town there is a double pool surrounded by five porticoes which is called Betsaida' (like many ancient writers he confused the name with that of the town in Galilee).[9] St Cyril, who was to become Bishop of Jerusalem, mentions at about the same time (AD 348) that the five porticoes mentioned by John are arranged in this way: 'Four surround the pool on all sides while the fifth one, in which the sick were waiting, went right through the middle'.[10]

Incidentally, the presence of these sick people also mentioned by John—'a large multitude of sick people were lying in the porches, blind, lame and paralysed people' (Jn 5:3)—has been explained by the finding of a small shrine to Aesculapius adjoining the pool. Aesculapius was the pagan God of Health.[11] This throws light on Jesus' warning to the paralysed man: 'Do not sin any more' (Jn 5:14). As a Jew the man was not supposed to seek for a miraculous cure in a pagan shrine![12]

All this confirms that John's description of the pool at Bethesda is remarkably accurate. If we take into account that the Fourth Gospel has been shown in *all* its fifteen main geographical references to have been precise and trust-worthy,[13] it follows that its traditions have to be treated with greater respect than they often have been by the critics. Even though the final edition of this gospel may have been composed towards the end of the first century, its contents reflect very ancient traditions that originated in Jerusalem.

The historian has supplied us with evidence from archaeology and ancient documents. Later we shall see that historical research also helps us to understand what happened on Easter day and how the gospel traditions were handed on. Historical research renders useful services. But this does not mean that the historian as historian can be the final judge of the truth of the Gospel's *religious* claims.

In fact, his observations, though helpful on one level, are somewhat irrelevant as far as the *message* of the gospel is concerned. 'The understanding of John's story does not in any way depend on an identification of the pool in question'.[14] Responding to the message the believer will rather reflect on his own sins, on God and healing.

> Bethesda's pool has lost its power!
> No angel, by his glad descent
> dispenses that divine endower
> which, with its healing waters, went;
> but He, whose word surpassed its wave,
> is still omnipotent to save.
>
> Bernard Barton

This then is the conclusion we may draw. The story of Jesus speaks about God; about what he has done for us in Jesus. Part of the story can be checked by historical research—the part that is rooted in human events. But to grasp the real message of the story and to accept its life-giving truth we have to be believers. Are we, perhaps, in need of historians who believe? This is not as absurd as you might think. Thoughtful historians admit that no history can be written as 'an objective study of neutral facts'. In selecting and assessing facts we are continuously applying our own interpretation. We look at history through the eyes of our culture and philosophy. We study the problems of the past as a key to those we face ourselves. Facts and interpretation are both essential. 'As any working historian knows, if he stops to reflect on what he is doing as he thinks and writes, the historian is engaged on a continuous process of moulding his facts to his interpretation and his interpretation to his facts'.[15] When studying the story of Jesus Christ we need to be open to the religious interpretation of what is being narrated.

What we have discussed so far applies in a special way to Jesus' resurrection. Is it an event that can be studied by historians? Has it left discernible traces in secular history? It is a question we need urgently to explore.

4
the RESURRECTION:
did anything really happen?

The resurrection is the central doctrine of our Christian faith. It has always been thus. From the earliest times the apostles preached Jesus as the one who had risen. It was what Peter told the Jewish authorities in Jerusalem: 'You killed the author of life, but God raised him from death' (Acts 3:15). 'Jesus Christ of Nazareth—whom you crucified but whom God raised from death!' (Acts 4:10). In fact, Jesus' resurrection was so central to the apostles' preaching that Paul could exclaim: 'If Christ has not been raised from death, then our message is useless, and so is your faith' (1 Cor 15:14).

An old profession of faith preserved in the New Testament begins as follows:

Christ died for our sins
    in accordance with the scriptures.
He was buried.
He was raised on the third day
    in accordance with the scriptures.
He appeared to Cephas, then to the Twelve.

(1 Cor 15:3-5)

This is an ancient creed, indeed. Paul recorded this fragment in the year AD 57, but he was obviously quoting a well-known formula whose contents, rhythmic form and stereotype expressions allow scholars to identify it as pre-Pauline and date it between AD 36 and 42.[16] 'Already, a few years after Jesus' death we have a fixed tradition, a formulated confession, that is a dogma, that was handed on in the communities and that functioned as a norm for the preaching of faith'.[17] 'The only reasonable conclusion is that what we have here is a doctrine fixed by the college of apostles in Jerusalem'.[18] The antiquity and universality of Christian faith in Jesus' resurrection cannot be doubted. But what about its historical truth?

The resurrection itself transcends history as we will see later. Anchored however as it is in ordinary history, certain claims can be probed by historical research. The early Christians held that Jesus' tomb was empty. He was believed to have risen 'on the third day'. Christians venerated the Sunday as the day of his resurrection. Let us consider each of these claims in turn.

Veneration of an empty tomb

The ancient creed stated: 'He was buried. He was raised . . .' Since the mention of burial implies a tomb, the profession of his rising implies that the tomb was believed to be empty. I am starting with this observation because it is very basic to the whole idea of resurrection for Jews. There have been modern theologians who claimed Jesus rose spiritually 'leaving his flesh and bones to rot in the grave'. To the Jews such a concept was impossible. To regain life involves both soul and body. It would be unthinkable for someone like Paul to proclaim the resurrection while the body was still in the tomb.[19] A claim that Jesus had risen would inevitably provoke the query: What about his tomb?

The tombs of great and holy men were visited and

venerated. Scripture itself lists a number of famous tombs: King David's (1 Kings 2:10), Solomon's (1 Kings 11:43), King Josiah's (2 Chron 35:24), the tombs of the Maccabean family (1 Mac 13:25-30), of Abraham and Jacob (Acts 7:15-16) and of John the Baptist (Mk 6:29). From literary sources and archaeological evidence a list has been drawn up of forty-nine well-known tombs in and around Jerusalem.[20] Jesus himself referred to the custom of venerating tombs (Mt 23:29-31). In such a climate both Jesus' disciples and his adversaries would have closely watched his tomb and taken an interest in whatever happened there.

When the gospel traditions speak of Jesus' tomb, they indicate a definite place that must have been known to everyone. 'In the place where he was crucified there was a garden and in the garden a new tomb where no one had ever been laid' (Jn 19:41). 'Joseph of Arimathea laid Jesus' body in his own new tomb which he had hewn in the rock; he rolled a great stone to the door of the tomb before leaving' (Mt 27:60). These are topographical details verifiable by anyone in Jerusalem.

Again, we know that in early Christian preaching at Jerusalem, as reflected in Acts, David and Jesus were compared. In Psalm 16:10 David had prayed, 'You will not abandon my soul to the underworld, nor allow your holy one to see corruption.' The early Christians maintained this verse did not apply to David, but to Jesus. 'Brethren,' Peter stated, 'I may say to you confidently of the patriarch David that he both died and was buried and his tomb is with us to this day. But being the prophet he was and knowing that God had promised under oath that he would set one of his descendants upon his throne, he foresaw and announced the resurrection of Christ, namely that it was he who was not to be abandoned to the underworld, whose flesh would not see corruption. This Jesus God has indeed raised up and of that we all are witnesses' (Acts 2:29-32).

Peter's argument only made sense because the undisturbed tomb of David could be contrasted with the empty tomb of Christ!

That is why all the four gospel accounts end with the finding of the empty tomb. It is impossible for me, in such a short essay, to analyse these stories here in detail. But just a few words are essential to indicate their origin and meaning. The oldest account, which we find in Mark 15:42—16:8, belongs to the ancient passion narrative. Internal analysis shows that this text was not used in kerygma (to proclaim the message) nor in apologetics (to defend one's faith). Rather it would seem to have been a liturgical reading which seems to have accompanied a ritual of reconstructing Jesus' passion in Jerusalem. This liturgical practice of the early Christian community had three parts which are reflected in the narrative: the vigil or night celebration (Mk 14:18-72), the Good Friday commemoration at the prayer hours (Mk 15:2-41) and the Easter celebration at the empty tomb (Mk 16:1-8). Succeeding events of the passion were linked to liturgical times of prayer: prime (Mk 15:1), terce (Mk 15:25), sext (Mk 15:33-34) and so on. Parts of the passion were re-enacted as is shown by visual presentations and dramatic elements.

This would explain how we have to understand the story of the women finding the tomb. No doubt, ancient historical events are preserved in the narration; yet the story itself reflects more directly liturgical practice. The women, representing Christian pilgrims, approach Jesus' tomb. They find the stone rolled away from its opening. They

Up, and away,
          thy SAVIOUR'S gone before,
why dost thou stay,
dull soul? behold the door
is open, and HIS precepts bid thee rise,
whose power hath vanquished all
                    thine enemies.
in vain thou say'st
thou are buried with thy SAVIOUR,
if thou delay'st
to show by thy behaviour,
that thou are risen with HIM.

                              Till thou shine
like HIM,
how can'st thou say HIS light is thine?

                    GEORGE HERBERT
                        1592 - 1633

enter the empty chamber and find a man clothed in white: the liturgical minister. The man preaches the Easter message: 'You seek Jesus of Nazareth who was crucified. He has risen. He is no longer here. See the place where they laid him.' What we have, therefore, is a very ancient record of liturgical practice directly linked to Jesus' tomb.[21]

Now we may never be able to verify some historical details recorded in the gospels: the names of the women who found the tomb empty (Lk 24:10) or the guard at the tomb (Mt 27:62-66); and the fact that the linen cloths that had covered Jesus were found intact (Jn 20:6-7). Such details may even have served theological purposes. What *is* incontrovertible, however, is the fact of the empty tomb itself. The apostles spoke of it. Pilgrims went to see it. It was there for people to inspect. Critics have tried to explain the fact of the empty tomb by conjecturing that Jesus' body had been stolen, or that he crawled out of his grave half-dead. Whatever we may think of such conjectures, one thing seems certain: Jesus' tomb was empty and the early Christians saw this as a confirmation of the fact that he had risen.

The third day

Not only the place of the resurrection, but also its exact time is recorded in ancient tradition. No less than twelve times we read in the New Testament that Jesus rose 'on the third day'.[22] A further nine times the parallel expression 'after three days' is used.[23] The expression occurs in Matthew, Mark, Luke, John, Acts and the letters of St Paul. We saw that it was already part of the ancient formula in Corinthians, 'He rose on the third day according to the scriptures' (1 Cor 15:4). What does the phrase mean?

Jesus was crucified on the Friday before the Passover. The Jews were anxious that Jesus should die before sunset, because the Passover feast began with sunset on the Friday evening and 'they did not want the bodies to stay on the crosses on the Sabbath for that Sabbath was a high feast' (Jn 19:31). For the same reason Joseph of Arimathea and Nicodemus were in a hurry to bury Jesus. 'Because it was the day before the Jewish Passover, they buried Jesus in the tomb since it was close at hand' (Jn 19:42). Counting from the Friday, 'the third day' was the Sunday. The Jews never used a mathematical calculation in these matters as we might do by thinking of three times twenty-four hours; they counted both the day of the start and the day of completion within the number. 'On the third day' or 'after three days' referred to: Friday, Saturday, Sunday. When they confessed that Jesus rose 'on the third day', they meant the date also referred to as 'the first day of the week' after the Passover (Mt 28:1; Mk 16:1-2; Lk 24:1; Jn 20:1).

This is a very precise dating of the event. In fact, at first sight the importance of this dating might escape us. Suppose for a moment that belief in the resurrection of Jesus arose some weeks or months after Jesus' crucifixion. We could then have simply expected them to proclaim that Jesus had risen. There would be no reason for them to claim it had happened on the third day. Some scholars have tried to find such a reason in the ancient formula: 'He rose on the third day *according to the scriptures*' (1 Cor 15:4). But the evidence does not support them. The reference 'according to the scriptures' refers to Jesus having to die and rise again as mainly found in Deutero-Isaiah (Is 52:13—53:12). There is no mention there of a 'third day'. In fact, there is no convincing Old Testament passage at all that could have occasioned the belief that Jesus had to rise on the third day. No single text is quoted for this purpose either in the New

Testament or in early Christian writings of the first two centuries. Jonah 2:1, which is sometimes referred to (see Mt 12:40), is a mismatch because the text says: 'After three days and three nights,' which is substantially different from 'on the third day'. Hosea 6:2, 'After two days he will revive us; on the third day he will raise us up,' belongs to a different context, is never quoted in the New Testament and can thus not have been the origin of the tradition.

Other explanations, such as that 'on the third day' would simply mean 'after a short time', or that corruption was supposed to occur within three days, could possibly explain its use in one or other text; it could never be the basis of such a definite and consistent confession, of such a precise dating. The constant and specific pointing to 'the third day' must contain the reminiscence of a historical event, of something that happened on the day after the Passover feast.[24] And, that 'first day of the week' happened to be a Sunday . . . .

Sunday as the Day of the Lord

We are so used to thinking of the Sunday as a special day, a day of worship and leisure, that we forget it had no special status at the time of Christ. For the Jews it was the Saturday, the Sabbath, that mattered as the day of rest. The 'first day of the week' was as uneventful and profane as Monday is for us. That same 'first day of the week' also had no significance for either the Hellenists or the Romans. But, surprisingly, the early Christians started to treat that day with special reverence. It was on the first day of the week that the early Christians came together to break the bread (Acts 20:7). It was then that they collected their common gifts (1 Cor 16:2). They called that day 'the day of the Lord' (Rev 1:10). The ancient instruction of the

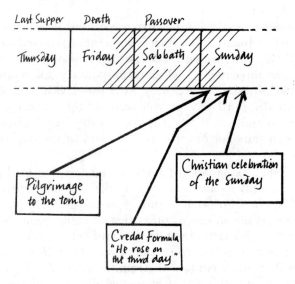

apostles of AD 100 says, 'On the Lord's Day you should come together, break the bread and give thanks, after having confessed your sins so that your sacrifice may be spotless' (Didache 14:1). St Ignatius of Antioch wrote in AD 110 that Christians were no longer celebrating the Sabbath, but lived under the observance of the Lord's Day 'on which also our own life is arisen through him and his death' (Magn 9:1). The same practice of Christian worship on the Sunday is attested by Pliny the Younger (AD 111-113) and by Justin Martyr in texts dating from AD 150. Why do we suddenly find among early Christians this observance of the Sunday as 'the Lord's Day'?

It is interesting to see the answer the gospels give to this question. Luke tells us that Jesus on that 'first day of the week' appeared to two disciples walking to Emmaus and broke the bread with them (Lk 24:28-32) and that on that same day Jesus appeared to the apostles in Jerusalem and celebrated the Eucharist with them (Lk 24:36-49). John speaks of a similar apparition to the disciples 'in the evening of that first day of the week' (Jn 20:19-23) and a further apparition precisely a week later (Jn 20:26-29). Peter says: 'God raised him up on the third day and made him appear, not to all people but to us who were chosen by him as witnesses, us who ate and drank with him after he rose from the dead' (Acts 10:40-41). The earliest sources therefore testify to the belief that Jesus appeared to the community of disciples on that first Sunday and that he celebrated the Eucharist with them.

This ties in extremely well with the Sunday practice recorded in other sources. These always indicate two reasons why Christians kept the Sunday: it was the day when Christ rose from the dead and it was the day when they came together for a eucharistic celebration. Now, it was well known that Jesus had actually instituted the Eucharist on a Thursday, on 'the night when he was betrayed' (1 Cor 11:23). What would have been more natural for them than to have selected the Thursday for the Eucharist? The fact that they did not do so, that from the earliest times on they decided to choose the Sunday; the fact also that, in spite of their strong Old Testament background they rejected the Sabbath for it, must point to an actual event of tremendous significance which took place on that Sunday, that first day of the week. This happening must have been linked to a eucharistic meal. In fact, no other explanation does justice to this sudden strong attachment of the Christian community to the Sunday Eucharist than to assume that the early community was convinced that they had actually met the risen Lord at a new eucharistic meal on that first Sunday. This meeting with the risen Christ was considered to be like a second institution of the Eucharist, which made Sunday forever the appropriate day for Christian worship and celebration.[25]

The events of Easter Day

I would like to come to an intermediate conclusion. The actual resurrection event is of such far-reaching significance that it transcends history. We will speak about this later. It is also interesting to note that the resurrection itself, since it goes beyond human observation, is not described in the Christian sources. They testify to its effects: the empty grave (to start with the least), encounters with the risen Christ, a total renewal of faith.

We asked the question: What can historical science say about the resurrection event? If we put together what we have seen so far, we can state that *on purely historical grounds* we have to admit that something unusual happened on that Sunday after the Passover. The tomb where Jesus had been buried was empty and became a place of pilgrimage. The early Christians were convinced Jesus had risen on that particular day, 'on the third day', and that he had appeared to them at the eucharistic meal so that from that time on it was the Sunday, not the Sabbath, that became the day of worship. It points to some profound *experience* that transformed them as a community.

No unbiased historians in my view can deny the fact of that experience. They may interpret it as a purely psychological event, as some form of mass hypnosis. Perhaps, understandably so. No one can accept the reality of the Christians' claim unless it makes sense within a totality of meaning. Before proceeding further we should therefore ask ourselves: Why bother about a man who died and is believed to have risen?

5

making sense of the RESURRECTION

I am not at all surprised that many historians refuse to give credence to the early Christians' claim that Jesus 'rose on the third day'. *No* amount of evidence would make them accept it. David Hume (1711-1776), that Scottish forerunner of modern historians, spoke for many when he wrote:

> Suppose that all the historians who treat of England should agree that on the first of January 1600 Queen Elizabeth died; that both before and after her death she was seen by her physicians and the whole court, as is usual with persons of her rank; that her successor was acknowledged and proclaimed by parliament; and that, after being interred a month, she again appeared, resumed the throne and governed England for three years: I must confess that I should be surprised at the concurrence of so many odd circumstances, but should not have the least inclination to believe so miraculous an event.[26]

Hume says it cannot be true, because such things do not happen; they do not make sense. In the case of Queen Elizabeth or any other ordinary person, he is right. But what if God uses such an unusual event as a *sign*? What if that sign precisely requires a new act of creation, a restoration of life?

In communication we rely heavily on signs. And signs, if we care to study them, prove remarkably unpredictable. Sounds and vocabulary in one language are complete gibberish in another. Gestures may convey one thing in one country, something else in the next. Signs need to be interpreted within a cultural context, within a totality of human experience. What seems nonsensical to us at first may suddenly become very meaningful in the light of genuine *experience*. A sign will only make sense to us if we experience it *as a sign*.

This brings us back to the experience of Jesus' disciples. We saw in the previous chapter that the Easter event left a visible imprint on the course of history by the ensuing veneration of the empty tomb and the introduction of the Sunday Eucharist. The impact of the resurrection experience becomes even more telling when we place the Easter event within a wider context. Jesus' crucifixion should have put an end to the small charismatic fellowship he had built up . . . Instead, a disillusioned and dispirited band of disciples suddenly turned into an enthusiastic and dynamic team of preachers. Pinchas Lapide, a well-known Jewish writer, recently expressed it so well in an interview.

> The resurrection is an invisible event that lies sandwiched between two certainties. The first certainty is the crucifixion. There is hardly a fact so well documented in Jesus' history as his death. And the other historical certainty is the foundation of the Church which first embraced the whole East, then spread the knowledge of God to nations until the ends of the earth. I find that one can assert on logical grounds that between the utter despair of the crucifixion and the emergence of the Church something very basic must have happened. The

explanation I find is the one given by the Jewish originators of the Church who point to the resurrection.[27]

Seeing the risen Christ

For the early Christians the most convincing sign that Jesus had risen was the fact that they actually saw him. Many apparitions of Jesus are recounted in the New Testament: to Mary Magdalene, to the women after they had left the tomb, to Peter, to the disciples on the road to Emmaus, to more than five hundred disciples on one occasion, to James, and, most of all, as we have seen, to the apostles assembled in the upper room on the first day of the week.

Without any doubt these encounters with the risen Christ were *real* to the disciples. They were happenings that shook them and transformed them. Yet they were not just like meeting an ordinary person of flesh and blood, like coming across someone in the street.

The apparition accounts stress the reality of Jesus' presence by narrating how he ate a piece of fish with them (Lk 24:36-43) and how Thomas could touch Jesus' wounds (Jn 20:27). These were exceptional gestures, however, not the rule; and they occur in later rather than earlier texts. The accounts show unmistakably that Jesus was different. Neither Mary Magdalene, nor the two disciples on the road to Emmaus, nor the apostles fishing on the Lake of Tiberias, recognised Jesus at first. The moment of recognition came as a surprise, as a mystical insight (Lk 24:31; Jn 20:16; 21:7). Jesus did not allow Mary to touch him or hold on to him (Jn 20:17). When he appeared to the assembled disciples, he entered the room through closed doors (Jn 20:19, 26). Jesus was not seen by Caiaphas or Pilate; he was only seen by believers. 'God raised him up on the third

because I have believed,
I bid my mind be still.
therein is now conceived
Thy hid yet sovereign will.

because I set all thought
                    aside in seeking Thee,
Thy proven purpose
    wrought abideth blest in me.
because I can no more exist
                    but in Thy being
blindly these eyes adore;
sightless are taught new seeing.

SIEGFRIED SASSOON
1886 - 1967

day and made him appear, not to all the people but only to us who were chosen by him as witnesses' (Acts 10:40-41). Jesus' apparitions were spiritual happenings that took place within the context of faith.

An encounter with Jesus came close to what we would call a 'vision' today. We can see this from the way in which Paul compares his own vision on the road to Damascus with the apparitions Peter, the Twelve, James and the five hundred disciples had (1 Cor 15:5-8). When Paul speaks about his own experience on the road to Damascus (Acts 26:12-18), he puts it on a line with a later vision he had in Jerusalem (Acts 22:17-21) and another vision he received in Troas (Acts 16:9-10). Seeing the Lord was a special kind of vision (1 Cor 9:1), different from other spiritual revelations and insights (2 Cor 12:1-4). But there was much they had in common too. Paul was an ecstatic visionary, a charismatic leader who had profound mystical experiences. Within those experiences the encounter with the risen Christ stood out as authoritative and unique.[28]

At this moment you may object that such visions are purely subjective and you can never prove that Jesus 'really' appeared. To some extent you would be right. Mystical experiences and spiritual visions do not come under the scope of direct scientific observation. But the fact that these visions are 'subjective' does not imply that they are purely imaginary and do not respond to reality. Reality goes far beyond what can be observed under the microscope, and seers of visions may see reality better than modern science ever can.[29] The apostles could see the risen Christ because, as Thomas Aquinas reminds us, 'they saw him alive with the eyes of faith'.[30]

The experiences which the apostles had of the risen Christ were of a very special kind, since they had to be the original witnesses of the resurrection. But other Christians, too, can share in this same experience. When we come to know and accept Jesus, it is not because of some notional assent, but because we have a living encounter with him. This is what Jesus promised. 'My Father will love whoever loves me. I too will love that person and reveal myself to him or her' (Jn 14:21). Jesus will show himself to us as the saviour, as the Lord, in a tangible manner. We will know he is there because we can see him. 'In a little while the world will see me no more, but you will see me' (Jn 14:19). Jesus' Spirit will speak to us, leading us into the fullness of truth (Jn 16:13). The confirmation of Jesus' resurrection is not, therefore, only the witness of a few individuals who lived nineteen centuries ago. By entering directly into our life and transforming it, Jesus will confirm his living presence in a very immediate and convincing spiritual experience.[31] It is this spiritual reality and the meaning it gives to our life that makes the resurrection such a central event.

The key fact in history

Allow me to enlarge a little on this question of meaning. People sometimes have very crude ideas about the resurrection. They imagine it means first and foremost that a corpse stepped out of the tomb and was subsequently seen by a number of people to speak and act. This is the 'animated corpse' concept of the resurrection. Small wonder that critics are sceptical and that historians claim such a happening must be both nonsensical and the product of pure imagination.

According to Christian faith, however, what changed at the resurrection is not only the body of Christ, but the situation in the world. We believe that at the resurrection

God was reconciled with sinful mankind. It was as if in a totally new creation he brought about a new situation in which there was hope and the prospect of eternal life. The resurrection is therefore a cosmic event. The apparitions of the risen Christ are a sign, confirming and announcing this event.

> The resurrection cannot be tamed or tethered by any utilitarian test. It is a vast watershed in history, or it is nothing. It cannot be tested for truth; it is the test for lesser truths. No light can be thrown on it; its own light blinds the investigator. It does not compel belief; it resists it. But once accepted as fact, it tells more about the universe, about history, and man's state and fate than all the mountains of other facts in the human accumulation.[32]

Let us go a little deeper into this meaning of the resurrection. Perhaps we could put it in this way. From the moment of our birth our life is threatened by death. When we leave the womb of our mother we lose a very basic security that we will never regain; but new possibilities for us as persons open up. The same happens when we leave our parental home. Throughout life we meet this combination of growth and loss. When a woman grows old she loses her fertility; a man loses his job. There is an aspect of dying in all this, with the possibility of greater freedom too. At the end of it all stands death itself. Will it mean a total destruction of our personality? Will it mean the loss of everything we have built up? Will our unique search, our specific individuality be dissolved into dust and ashes for ever?

The resurrection provides the Christian answer to this universal problem of our existence. The resurrection is the fact that can fundamentally alter the negative character of our common human death.[33] The resurrection is the possibility for us as specific persons in our concrete situation to release ourselves from whatever in the past or present obstructs us from being truly ourselves and to embrace the fullness of life.[34] The confession that Jesus Christ has risen is for the Christian an expression of the certainty that otherwise would seem only a beautiful dream, that love is stronger than death.[35]

> Jesus rose to definitive life, a life no longer subject to chemical and biological laws. He stands outside the possibility of dying, in the Eternity given by love ... Whoever confesses the ultimate meaning of Jesus, confesses at the same time his meaning as the one who defeats death, his lordship over death, his resurrection.[36]

This is no empty talk. It means that if we share in Jesus' resurrection, our everyday life takes on a new quality. We experience what Paul called 'the power of his resurrection' (Phil 3:10).

The resurrection can thus be said to be truly transcendent. It belongs to history because it is rooted in it and transforms it. Pope Paul VI could call it 'the unique and sensational event on which the whole of human history turns'.[37] Yet it goes beyond the confines of ordinary history. 'It truly is a primal miracle', he tells us, 'which transcends history and so is beyond the reach of historical enquiry ... The reality of the resurrection of Jesus lies beyond our earthly categories.'[38]

If Jesus' resurrection can thus be shown to be eminently meaningful, how does this relate to his message? Have his teachings been faithfully recorded? Can he become my personal guide?

6

can we trust the gospels?

In the gospels Jesus is reported to have said that any disciple who treasures his teachings and shapes his life according to them is like a wise man who built his house on rock. 'The rain poured down, floods overwhelmed it and the gale beat against it. But it will not fall because it had been built on rock' (Mt 7:25). Since Jesus is my teacher whose resurrection gives a totally new meaning to my life, his teachings are a precious gift that I value highly. But can I be sure that what I find in the gospel texts are the genuine teachings of my Master?

Since the Enlightenment many doubts have been thrown on the reliability of the gospel traditions. The critics who express such doubts will commonly admit that Jesus was a preacher who lived and died in Palestine, but they maintain that few of his original words have come down to us intact. We have some fragments of Jesus' teaching, they will contend, fragments which have been enlarged and re-interpreted by his disciples. Moreover, to corroborate the disciples' belief in Jesus' salvific death and divinity, many so-called sayings of Jesus were 'created' by the early Christian community and attributed to Jesus himself. If we were to believe these critics, it is not the original Jesus who is speaking to us in the gospels, but rather the divinized product of collective imagination.

What should we make of these allegations? Can we disprove them? Can we show that the teachings presented in the gospels do go back to Jesus himself?

I believe we can. We will first study the attitude of the evangelists, the writers of the gospels. Then we will look at the trustworthiness of the written documents and oral traditions which they used as sources. Finally, we will consider the importance of eyewitness accounts.

The message of a foreword

Before we judge the work of the evangelists by scrutinizing what they actually do, it is only fair to listen to what they say about their intentions. Luke for one tells us in so many words that he has studied the facts and wants to present an accurate report. Telling us the truth about Jesus is his declared purpose.

> Many writers have undertaken before now
> to compose accounts of the events
> which took place among us,
> in harmony with the tradition
> which the original eyewitnesses
> and ministers of the gospel
> have handed down to us.
> Therefore, most excellent Theophilus,
> I too decided
> to write an orderly account of it for you,
> after investigating everything carefully from the beginning.
> It is my aim that you should recognise
> the reliability of the oral instruction you received.
>
> Lk 1:1-4

This seems very plain speaking. Luke says that he has studied his material carefully, checking out its truthfulness with eyewitnesses and the original preachers of the gospel. He assures his reader that he wants to present fact not fiction. Unless he is deliberately trying to deceive, he claims that his gospel is just the opposite of what the critics make it out to be: it is a reliable report, not a compilation of later inventions. The critics, for example, say that Jesus'[38] announcements of his own death and resurrection as salvific events were never spoken by the original Jesus; they were created by the later community.[39] Luke, however, asserts that Jesus made these announcements at least seven times in his gospel.[40] Either the critics are wrong, or Luke is presenting his gospel under false pretences.

But the solution may be much simpler, you might argue. Perhaps Luke *was* claiming to give a factual report but he did not mean a factual report as we would understand it. At that time the science of history had not yet been invented. People had no idea of what accuracy in reporting means. Belonging to the pre-scientific age, they would so easily mix legends and anecdotes with proved facts. Making up stories, you might say, is just part of the way they wrote history in those times!

It is true that the evangelists were theologians as well as historians. They expressed certain truths in literary forms we would not use today, as I will explain in chapter 8. It's also true that they were not as concerned as we are today with descriptive detail or accidental circumstances. In that sense their way of reporting *was* different from ours today.

But to say that they had no idea of history writing, of factual reporting, of accuracy in conveying the substance of historical events, would be a serious mistake. Both Jews and Hellenists knew what scientific research involves. They realised that an ideal historian should be faithful to his sources, critical in judgement and unprejudiced in his presentation. They were interested in the accuracy and historical reliability of the reports they read. Even if some historians at the time fell below standard—as many do today—the value of establishing historical certainties was clearly in their minds.

The matter is so important that we should discuss it at some length. Ancient writers often testify to the need to narrate the facts as they happened. Herodotus (450 BC), Thucydides (460-400 BC), Polybius (200-118 BC), Dionysius (60-30 BC), Lucian of Samosata (AD 125-180), Cicero (106-43 BC) and Flavius Josephus (AD 37-100) discussed and set out the standards by which historical reports should be judged. Dionysius, for example, condemns histories 'written in an offhand or negligent manner', and Cicero may be quoted as representing common conviction when he said:

> Who does not know history's first law to be that an author must not dare to tell anything but the truth? And its second that he must make bold to tell the whole truth? That there must be no suggestion of partiality in his writings? Nor of malice?[41]

Thucydides declares that historians should depend on eyewitness accounts and original documents. He defines his method as follows:

> With reference to the narration of events, far from permitting myself to derive it from the first source that came to hand, I did not even trust my own impressions, but it rests partly on what I saw myself, partly on what others saw for me, the accuracy of the report being always tried by the most severe and detailed tests possible. My conclusions have cost me

some labour from the want of coincidence between accounts of the same occurrences by different eye-witnesses, arising sometimes from imperfect memory, sometimes from undue partiality for one side or the other.[42]

Other historians, Herodotus, Polybius, Lucian, Sallust (86-35 BC), Tacitus and Josephus, profess the same ideal and at times mention such primary sources as were available to them.

The quotation from Thucydides illustrates also that ancient historians recognised the difference between mere tradition and accurate history writing. The importance of carefully sifting the source material is stressed by Herodotus, Polybius and Josephus. Lucian lays down this rule:

As to the facts themselves, the historian should not assemble them at random, but only after much laborious and painstaking investigation. He should for preference be an eyewitness, but, if not, listen to those who tell the more impartial story, those whom one would suppose least likely to subtract from the facts or add to them out of favour or malice.[43]

A special study has shown that modern scholars judge several of the ancient historians to be trustworthy and accurate in the writings which they left us. They give full marks to Herodotus, Thucydides, Polybius and Tacitus; Josephus, Caesar, Polybius and Livy pass with more than average. The study concludes: 'The fact that in the first centuries many historians wrote carelessly does not imply that the early Christian writers must have had no idea what accurate writing involved'.[45]

The question of historicity *did* mean something for the

contemporaries of the apostles. When Luke in his prologue stresses that he made careful investigations and that he aims at proving the reliability of the stories and teaching that up to then had not been written down, his claims were meaningful to his readers. They expected historical truthworthiness, and nothing less would satisfy them.

Of course, Luke did not intend to write history *as such*. His purpose was to report accurately the instruction given by the Master. Careful comparison with other prologues to Greek writings at the time shows that Luke's foreword is most like those written to preface manuals of instruction.[46] Such manuals were functional and matter of fact. They derived directly from a teaching context: they are the written deposit of the *techne* or skill, the distillation of the teaching of a school or a craft tradition as it was passed down from one generation to another. Physicians, metal workers, weavers and other craftsmen used such manuals to learn and pass on the knowledge of their skill. We know now that many of the early Christians belonged to the middle classes: small business men, skilled labourers, people owning their own workshop. 'The typical Christian was a free artisan or small trader.'[47] Luke the physician and Paul the tentmaker could speak to them in their own language. Luke consciously presented his report of Jesus' teaching in the form of an instructional manual which was supposed to be sober in style, to the point and reliable in its teaching.

No teacher like Jesus

Whereas Luke wrote for Hellenists, Matthew composed his Gospel for Jews. Nevertheless, the same intention of accuracy and truthfulness is clear from his presentation.

Matthew presents Jesus mainly as a teacher, a *rabbi*.

When thou turn'st away from ill
Christ is this side of thy hill.

When thou turnest toward good
Christ is walking in thy wood.

When to love is all thy wit,
Christ doth at thy table sit.

When God's will is thy heart's pole,
then is CHRIST thy very soul.

GEORGE MACDONALD

1824 - 1905

He arranges his Gospel around five sermons of Jesus (chapters 5-7; 10; 13; 18 and 24-25). In these sermons he has put together various teachings of Jesus in a systematic form. As Moses proclaimed the Ten Commandments and the other laws from Mount Sinai, so did Jesus, according to Matthew, proclaim his Beatitudes and liberating teachings as the start of God's new kingdom.

Matthew also records sayings of Jesus himself that show that there has been no other teacher as important as Jesus was.

> Do not allow yourselves to be called *rabbi,* for you have only one teacher, and you are all brethren ... Neither allow yourselves to be called masters, for you have but one master, the Christ.
>
> Mt 23:8-10

> Heaven and earth will pass away, but my words will not pass away.
>
> Mt 24:35

> Everyone who hears these words of mine and does not put them into practice will be like a fool who built his house on sand.
>
> Mt 7:26

> Whoever denies me before other people, I will deny before my Father who is in heaven.
>
> Mt 10:33

> To me has been given all authority in heaven and on earth. Go therefore and make disciples of all nations, baptising them in the name of the Father and of the Son and of the Holy Spirit, and teaching them to observe all that I have told you.
>
> Mt 28:18-20

What could be worse than for a disciple to adulterate the teachings of his Master? In the Old Testament Moses warned repeatedly: 'You may not add to the word which I command you, nor detract from it' (Dt 4:2); 'Be careful to put into practice everything I command you. Do not add to it or detract from it' (Dt 13:1). The author of the book of Revelations pronounced a curse on anyone who would dare to add to his words or take away from them (Rev 22:18-19).[43]

Since for Matthew Jesus is the greatest teacher of all, how would he ever dare to invent new teaching and ascribe it to his Master or give a new slant to his Master's words to make them fit his own understanding? How could he ever presume to know things better than his Master had? We can be sure that Matthew was convinced that the teaching contained in his Gospel was a faithful rendering of what the actual historical Jesus had taught.

Accepting the evangelists' good intention, however, is not enough. Do we have some independent means to check out the reliability of their accounts? Can we find corroborating evidence to support their claims?

7
what did JESUS really say?

The gospels of Matthew, Mark and Luke were manuals of instruction. It is important for us to recognise this. If a biographer today wants to write a life of, say, Churchill, he will study the sources, but the final presentation will be his own. The evangelist did not have this freedom. The bulk of his writing had already been done in the 'traditions' that lay before him: stories, parables, sayings of Jesus, disputes with the scribes. The evangelist could change the order, explain certain words or events, add his commentary, present the material in a logical form; he could not deviate from the given traditions themselves.

To understand what this means, let us look at one such tradition as we find it in each of the three gospels (please note that we print here very exact translations of the original Greek so that variations in wording can be compared).

Matthew:

When they deliver you up, do not be anxious how you are to speak or what you are to say; for what you are to say will be given to you in that hour. For it is not you who will speak but the Spirit of your Father speaking through you.

Mt 10:19-20

Mark:
When they bring you to trial and deliver you up, do
not be anxious beforehand what you are to say; but
say whatever is given you in that hour. For it is not
you who will speak but the Holy Spirit.

Mk 13:11

Luke:
When they bring you before the synagogues and the
rulers and the authorities, do not be anxious how or
what you are to answer or what you are to say. For
the Holy Spirit will teach you in that very hour what
you have to say.

Lk 12:11-12

Reading the three versions of this tradition we cannot
fail to see that, in spite of small variations, they go back
to one original text. The same tradition, incidentally, is
found in a slightly alternative rendering in Lk 21:14-15 and
Jn 14:26. Since such a tradition forms a unit, we speak of
it as a 'passage' or 'pericope'. We can study such a passage
on its own merits, try to determine its origin, see if it can
be traced back to Jesus.

How much of the gospels is made up of such traditional
material? The answer is: Practically all of it. Take, for
instance, Matthew's gospel. Its total of 18,518 words in
the original Greek text comprises 196 passages. Of these
passages 100 are parallel to both Mark and Luke (7,678
words). Matthew has 49 passages in common with Luke
alone (4,923 words). 47 passages are found only in Matthew
(5,917 words), but even these passages can be shown to
have an earlier origin. In other words, all Matthew did was
to present traditions that already existed, arranging them
in a particular way and adding his explanations here and
there.

You might think that the evangelists simply copied from each other. The outcome of more than a hundred years of painstaking research seems to rule this out. Rather, scholars have deduced from the common passages the existence of written sources that pre-date the gospels. These were collections of 'traditions' from which the evangelists drew when they composed their gospels. The two main written documents which it is thought must have existed are referred to as 'UrMark', known to Matthew, Mark and Luke, and 'Quelle', drawn upon by Matthew and Luke.

However, what is even more interesting is that it has also been shown that the traditions, before they were written down in these documents, had been handed down in oral tradition. Such oral tradition should not be confused with the rumours, popular small talk or family traditions found in our own society. We are talking here about precise texts that were formulated by a teacher and memorised by the disciples. We will explain this better further on, but in general we may say that oral instruction learned by heart would present precisely those features that are so prominent in the gospel traditions: repetition of very exact phrases with a certain amount of free formulation. If you look at the samenesses and differences of the three versions of the tradition printed above, you will see that the key idea remains the same: Do not be anxious—the Spirit will help you say the right thing. Slight variations between them, however, occur, such as 'the Spirit of your Father'/'the Holy Spirit', exactly as one would expect in texts that have been learnt by heart.

Tracing the gospel traditions

It will not be easy for me to condense in a short space the enormous volume of research that has been done in tracing the traditions to their source. The evangelists claim that Jesus was their author, the Master from whom they derive their authority.

Perhaps it is necessary at this stage to remind ourselves of how Jesus, as a Jewish rabbi, used to teach. At the end of each instruction Jesus used to formulate a summary of it in a brief poetic form. 'The conclusion of a doctrinal instruction was a phrase which the disciples received and which they repeated until it was indelibly imprinted in their memory'.[48] 'The final result of what might have been a lengthy doctrinal instruction was formulated in a thesis that contained the worthwhile conclusion. This thesis was memorised and handed on, not the whole instruction.'[49] A good disciple was someone who 'understands easily and forgets with difficulty'; 'a plastered cistern which loses not a drop.'[50]

To help memorization Jesus formulated his teaching in a distinctive way, in the style of prophetic oracles. His sayings would follow the rhythmic qualities of poetry. We find in them Hebrew parallelism, the repetition of refrains, ring-construction, alliteration and the rise and fall of accents. Jesus' sayings were also formulated as dramatically as possible. Question and answer, short colourful descriptions, puns, dynamic actions: all dramatic means of expression were utilised to create a vivid picture that could almost be enacted. Frequently, mnemotechnical or mnemonic helps were inserted by him, that is, devices to help the memory, for example, key words, refrains, grouping passages under one linking phrase, rhyme and the numbering of passages.[51]

Jesus' instruction was expressed in Aramaic. We know this because the Greek text of the Gospel traditions abounds with Aramaicisms: idioms and constructions proper to

Aramaic, not to Greek.[52] Often the variation between a tradition's form in one or the other gospel can be explained best by the Aramaic underlying oral tradition. Compare these lines:

> Teacher, what *good* must I do . . .?
> > (didaskale, ti agathon) Mt 19:16

> *Good* teacher, what must I do . . .?
> > (didaskale agathe, ti) Mk 10:17

> *Good* teacher, what must I do . . .?
> > (didaskale agathe, ti) Lk 18:18

The phrase is taken from the tradition of the rich young man, a passage found in UrMark and used by all three evangelists. In its Greek form the wording is so different that confusion is excluded: *didaskale ti agathon* (teacher what good) and *didaskale agathe, ti* (good teacher what). But in Aramaic the difference is only found in where a *pause* is put:

> *Rabbi—tob ma zeh* (Teacher—good what is it . . .?)

> *Rabbi tob—ma zeh* (Teacher the good—what is it . . .?)

It proves at the same time both the Aramaic origin and its original formulation in *oral* tradition.

A further study of the contents of the traditions reveals that they must have originated in Palestine. Scores of Palestinian names of places are firmly embedded within the traditions: Capernaum, Bethsaida, the Lake of Galilee, Naim, Jericho, the land of the Gerasenes, and many others. Moreover, the traditions presuppose customs unknown to Hellenists but characteristic of Jewish Aramaic society: the leper has to bring a sacrifice of purification (Mt 8:4), the woman with the 'flow of blood' is ritually impure (Mk 5:33), Jesus has frequent disputes about the Sabbath and is called 'the Son of David' (Mt 20:30 etc.), the disciples have to pay Temple tax (Mt 17:24). The miracle accounts presuppose the Old Testament background, such as stilling the storm (God created the sea), multiplying the bread (the manna in the desert), raising people to life (see Elijah and Elisha), curing the blind and paralysed (as foretold by the prophets). All such examples—and these are but a few of them—point unmistakably to a *Palestinian* origin of the traditions.

Now we know that the Jewish people revolted against the Romans from AD 66-70, which led to their utter defeat and the destruction of Jerusalem. Archaeologists tell us that for many years afterwards there seems to have been no settlement in Jerusalem and that life was disrupted throughout Palestine. The Jewish Christian community too was scattered even before the siege, as we read in Eusebius' *History of the Church.* This, then, gives us the latest possible date for the formulation of the traditions.

> The authentic early topographical colouring in the gospels, together with the strong evidence of an Aramaic substratum point inescapably to a date before the catastrophe of AD 66-70 for the formation of the gospel tradition. . . . In the writer's opinion there is scarcely a passage in the gospels which was appreciably influenced in formulation by the history of the Church in the decades immediately following the year AD 70.[53]

Can we pinpoint the time of formulation even more precisely? We can. It is clear that some narrative traditions were formulated after the resurrection. For instance, the Passion account and the apparition stories could only have been formulated at that time. Also some of the miracle accounts may have received their earliest expression in this period when the apostles began to proclaim what Jesus had done. When Peter was instructing Cornelius for baptism he told him: 'You must have heard about Jesus of Nazareth, how God poured out on him the Holy Spirit and power. He went everywhere, doing good and healing all who were under the power of the devil, for God was with him. We are witnesses of everything that he did in the land of Israel and in Jerusalem' (Acts 10:38-39). We can be sure that Peter would amplify such a statement with a description of various healings and other miracles that Jesus had performed. We call such a baptismal instruction the 'setting in life' in which traditional teaching was formulated.

We can be sure, however, that the actual teachings of Jesus had been formulated much earlier, during Jesus' ministry itself. For we know that the apostles were sent out to preach even before Jesus' resurrection. The sending of the apostles is frequently mentioned in ancient passages.[54] Many ancient traditions are anchored in such a sending: such as the advice about what to take along on the journey (Mk 6:7-9), the prayer for labourers in God's harvest (Mt 9:37), the saying 'I send you as sheep among wolves' (Lk 10:3), the encouragement to speak boldly (Mt 10:26-27), and so on. Incidents were recorded of how the disciples failed (Mt 17:14-16), or how they reported success (Lk 10:17). But *what* did they preach?

Since the apostles were 'sent'—for this is what the name 'apostle' means—they were not preaching their own inventions. The substance of their message could only have been the prophetic teaching they had received from Jesus. Jesus must have prepared them for this task by providing rather precise formulations, such as other rabbis did. In other words, here we have the original 'setting in life' in which Jesus' prophetic oracles, his parables, his replies to

Wide fields of corn along the valleys spread;
the rain and dews mature the swelling vine;
I see the LORD is multiplying bread;
I see him turning water into wine;
I see him working all the works divine
he wrought when Salemward his steps were led;
the selfsame miracles around him shine;
he feeds the famished; he revives the dead;
he pours the flood of light on darkened eyes;
he chases tears, diseases, fiends away;
his throne is raised upon these orient skies;
his footstool is the pave whereon we pray.
Ah, tell me not of CHRIST in Paradise,
for he is all around us here today.

JOHN CHARLES EARLE
1601 – 1665

the Pharisees and scribes, his announcements of the Kingdom and God's judgement were formulated. It is this which gave rise to the first and oldest collection of oral tradition. We can also be sure that this earliest collection already included some narrative sections. Did the apostles not have to explain what Jesus had done? How he drove out demons? How he could heal people? How his own behaviour was in harmony with his teaching?[55]

The overall consistency of Jesus' teaching as recorded in the gospel traditions also confirms that they were formulated by Jesus himself. A large group can criticise a draft; it cannot produce one that is uniform in thought and style. The camel, as the saying goes, is a horse invented by a committee. Even less can the enthusiasm of a charismatic leader be replaced by the response of his followers. Jesus' captivating personality, his distinctive teachings, his typical utterances and parables, his characteristic way of acting is so uniform in the passages, documents and gospels that only Jesus himself, the original prophetic leader, could have given them this personal touch. We cannot explain the rays of the sun if we take away the sun itself.[56]

In the previous chapter we saw that the evangelists intended to give a reliable account of Jesus' teaching. In this chapter we have studied copious evidence to substantiate that claim. The traditions contained in the gospels *do* go back to Jesus himself and the immediate circle of disciples who were eyewitnesses to all he said and did. But did everything narrated in the gospels happen exactly as stated? Did the evangelists write as we write today? We will discuss this in the next chapter.

8
how to read the gospels

Our studies so far have shown that the evangelists were determined to give us a truthful account about Jesus and that they could base their report on accurate sources. As loyal disciples they wanted to present the teaching of the Master as faithfully as possible. We should remember, however, that they lived two thousand years ago and belonged to a different culture. In their presentation they followed the conventions of their own people. Critics of the gospels have sometimes overlooked this, and accused the evangelists of inaccuracy or even deception.

Take for example the gospel of Matthew. We have already seen how important Jesus' teaching is for Matthew. A study of the contents of the gospel bears this out. Matthew arranged the whole of Jesus' life around five key sermons: the sermon on the mount (Mt 5-7), the apostolic sermon (Mt 10), the sermon of parables (Mt 13), the hierarchical sermon (Mt 18) and the sermon on the Last Things (Mt 24-25). Comparing Matthew's narration with that of the other evangelists we find that he often shortens parts of the story, never Jesus' teaching. Matthew preserved fourteen parables and instructions of Jesus which we do not find in the other gospels. Passing on Jesus' words without changing one dot or one iota is his aim (Mt 5:18).

Yet he did not do this in a simplistic or naive fashion. The sermon on the mount, which Matthew presents as if Jesus spoke it all on one occasion (Mt 5:1-2; 7:28-29), is made up of thirty-one distinct teachings of Jesus which, as we can see from the other gospels, in reality Jesus taught on many separate occasions. By putting them altogether in one sermon Matthew did not want to claim that they had all been spoken by Jesus on one and the same day. He wanted to show that all these various teachings together make up a comprehensive set of instructions regarding sanctity in Jesus' kingdom. He knew that people in his time would understand it in this way. By making a mountain the setting for Jesus' teaching on sanctity, he deliberately compared it with the proclamation of the Old Testament code of laws on Mount Sinai. The presentation therefore had a *theological* meaning; it served to bring out the importance of Jesus' teaching.

Or consider the list of Jesus' ancestors with which Matthew opens his gospel. Such lists were common in Matthew's time. Most Jews were anxious to be able to prove their descent from orthodox parents. In Jesus' case it also served to link him to David; everyone knew that the Messiah was to be a descendant of David's.

Matthew, however, presents the list in a peculiar fashion. He presents the list in three sections: fourteen generations from Abraham to David; fourteen from David to the Exile; and fourteen from the Exile to Jesus himself (Mt 1:1-17). To arrive at this number fourteen Matthew had to allow himself certain liberties. For instance, between the ancestors Joram and Azariah, he omits Ahaziah, Joash and Amaziah.[57] Similar omissions can be seen in other places. In other words, Matthew deliberately mentioned only three times fourteen ancestors. The question is: Why?

It was customary in his day to reflect on the inner meaning of names. Since Jesus was eminently 'the Son of David', Matthew focussed on the name 'David'. In theological speculation of the time 'David' had the numerical value of 'fourteen'.[58] 'Seven' is for the Jews the number of blessing, and 'fourteen' is thus broken up as 'two times seven'. By presenting Jesus' list of ancestors as three times fourteen generations, that is, six times seven generations, Matthew was drawing the attention of his readers to the fact that with Jesus Christ a new supreme blessing began, namely the seventh of a series of seven generations.

Matthew's readers knew perfectly well that this was a *theological* construction. In their eyes Matthew was not distorting facts or falsifying the figures (which were perfectly well known from other parts of Scripture anyway). They understood the artistic and spiritual meaning of his presentation.

Stories for reflection

To do justice to the gospels we have to keep this element of presentation constantly in mind. The story of the temptation of Jesus in the desert by the devil, for example, has been seriously misunderstood in later times. It was thought by some that Matthew narrated these temptations as hard facts. That he claimed Jesus had actually met the devil in person and had been arguing with him from scripture. When Matthew says that the devil took Jesus to Jerusalem and made him stand on the parapet of the temple, or again that the devil took Jesus to a very high mountain and showed him all the kingdoms of the world, they imagined he was claiming these were actual physical events. If they had only known Jewish literature, they would never have made such a mistake.

To grasp the significance of the temptation story we have to go back to the Old Testament account of Abraham's sacrifice. It will be remembered that God appeared to Abraham and asked him to bring his son Isaac as a sacrifice on Mount Moriah (Gen 22:1-19). The story is very dramatic. Abraham actually takes Isaac with him on a donkey, travels for three days to Moriah, climbs with his son to the top of the mountain, binds his son on a makeshift altar and prepares him for the sacrifice. Only at the last moment, when he lifts his knife, God stops him and praises his obedience.

We now know that this story fascinated the Jews of Jesus' time. A special day of commemoration had been instituted which was called 'the binding of Isaac'. Meditations were composed on Abraham's state of mind and on Isaac's readiness to die. Sermons were preached on the topic, special prayers and intercessions composed. Much attention was devoted to Abraham's unswerving loyalty to God. And it was asked: Was Abraham during the time of preparation for the sacrifice not tempted to go against God's command?

Thus a famous meditation arose, in a form known as *midrash* in Aramaic. This is an elaboration of one scripture passage in the light of other scripture texts. Because of its frequent occurrence in Jewish spiritual writings we can reconstruct more or less how this particular *midrash* arose.

First of all, it was recognised that God gave Abraham the unusual command in order to test him. Implicit and explicit comparisons were made with the temptations of Job.[59]

In the next stage it was pointed out how confusion and doubt could easily arise in Abraham's mind. Notice in the following extract from the *midrash* at this stage of its development how Abraham's temptation is presented as a *thought;* and how both his tempting thought and the reply to the temptation are clothed in biblical quotations:

> Abraham prayed to God and said: 'You know that when you told me, ''Take your only son Isaac and offer him for a burnt offering,'' it was in my heart to answer, ''Yesterday you told me, 'In Isaac shall your offspring be called' (Gen 17:19), and today you order me to offer him up as a burnt offering.'' But although I could have answered in that manner, I suppressed my inclination, and did not do so, as it is said, ''as a dumb man who opens not his mouth'' (Ps 38:13).'[60]

In a further development the same *midrash* was told, but now the doubts of Abraham were attributed to the devil. In the following excerpt Satan carries the name Samael.

> Samael came to see our father Abraham and said to him: 'Old man, old man, have you lost your senses? Are you going to kill a son who was granted to you when you were a hundred years old?'
> 'Certainly,' Abraham said.
> 'And if God should impose still more severe tests upon you will you be able to endure them?'
> 'I will,' he answered, 'even stronger ones than this.'
> Samael continued: 'But tomorrow God will say to you: ''Shedder of blood! You are guilty of having shed the blood of your son.'''
> 'Even so,' said Abraham, 'I must obey'.[61]

Finally the *midrash* received its definitive form.

According to this the devil tempted Abraham three times. Each time he tempted Abraham by quoting from the Bible and each time Abraham answered in biblical quotations.

> While Abraham was on the way to carry out this divine command, Satan met him and said: 'Why must grievous trials be inflicted upon you? Behold you have instructed many, and you have strengthened the weak hands. Your word has supported him that was falling, and now this unfair burden is laid upon you' (see Job 4:2-5).
>
> Abraham answered: 'I will walk in my integrity' (Ps 26:11).
>
> Then Satan said: 'Is not the fear of God your folly? Please, remember the verse, "Whoever perished innocent?" (Ps 37:25).' Then, finding that he could not persuade Abraham, he said: 'Now a word came to me secretly. I overheard behind the veil in the holy of holies (see Job 4:2): "A lamb will be the sacrifice and not Isaac."'
>
> Abraham replied: 'A liar deserves not to be believed even when he speaks the truth'.[62]

The *midrash* of the three temptations of Abraham became so well known and was used in so many different forms that it gave rise to similar temptation stories in reflections on other great men. Thus we find temptation stories featuring Isaac, Moses, David, Samson and so on. It had become a common form of meditation, a popular way of reflecting on how great men had to overcome internal doubts and struggles when serving God. People knew that putting the words into the mouth of Satan was just a manner of speaking. What counted was the underlying conviction: the hero in question *could* have objected in this or that manner, but he remained faithful to the task given by God.

Knowing this literary form helps us understand the story of Jesus' temptations. Matthew's contemporaries, when hearing the story, would understand immediately that there is no question of the devil meeting Jesus physically, of him taking Jesus to the pinnacles of the Temple or transporting him to a high mountain. What was at stake was Jesus' fidelity to his mission. While Jesus was preparing himself in the desert for the beginning of his mission he would naturally have been 'tempted' to use money, power, good publicity and so on to help him. Jesus, however, decided that his true strength should derive from God's own words and that he should rely solely on spiritual means.

This is the whole meaning of the temptation story; and what a powerful message it is! It is very likely that Jesus himself confronted the apostles with this *midrash* when they, perhaps, urged him to build up a fund of money, become a secular king, or begin to collect an army. But whether the original formulation in this case was Jesus' own or goes back to a meditation of Jesus' close disciples its meaning for contemporary readers was clear: instead of relying on secular forms of power, Jesus remained true to the true spiritual character of his mission.

There are at least three other examples of *midrash* in Matthew's gospel. The story of the Magi is a meditation on Jesus' origin and destiny based on seven Old Testament prophecies.[63] The Transfiguration (Mt 17:1-8) reflects an ecstatic vision of Jesus in which he understood himself as the new Moses and the new Elijah.[64] The catch of a fish with a coin in its mouth contains elements of a moral tale well known in rabbinical circles. It may well be that in all these cases reflections and instructions by Jesus, or by his closest disciples, were presented in narrative form.

Editorial pruning

It should also be remembered that the evangelists, like writers of all times, had to condense their presentation by cutting out details and focussing on what was essential.

A dramatic hijack lasting twenty hours is telescoped by journalists into an 800-word report. This means: simplifying, cutting short, omitting a lot of details. Matthew often does the same. The Roman officer, whose slave was ill, *sent friends* to Jesus to intercede on his behalf (Lk 7:1-10). Matthew, however, omits the friends and tells the story as if the Roman officer approached Jesus himself (Mt 8:5-13). According to the old tradition Jesus gave complicated instructions to two of his disciples on how to find the room for the last supper; they had to follow a man carrying a jug of water and so on (Mk 14:12-14). Matthew simplifies by making Jesus say: 'Go to a certain man in the city' (Mt 26:18). In the discussion on the greatest commandment, one of the scribes maintains it is love of God and of the neighbour; Jesus expresses wholehearted approval (Lk 10:25-28). Matthew omits mention of the scribe and attributes the saying directly to Jesus (Mt 22:34-40).

A present-day historian might find such details interesting, if not important; for Matthew they were a distraction, not a help. We should keep this in mind when judging Matthew's accuracy in the famous passage concerning the curse of the fig tree. Ancient tradition had it that Jesus cursed the fig tree on one day (Mk 11:12-14) and that it had withered on the next (Mk 11:20-21). Since Matthew compresses all clashes concerning the Temple into one big day of conflict, he shortens the happenings around the fig tree by saying: 'At once the fig tree dried up' (Mt 21:19). This is not a distortion of the facts in order to make a miracle seem greater, as some critics have claimed. It is Matthew's way of reporting the substance of what happened, rather than the detail.

This loyalty to substance rather than to accidentals also explains why Matthew, in spite of his great respect for Jesus' words, will occasionally enlarge on what Jesus had said in order to make their meaning clear to his readers. Matthew was, after all, a teacher in the early Church. He had a pastoral concern. He was not a stenographer recording empty phrases; he was a preacher passing on the living words of the greatest teacher that had ever taught.

In the 'Our Father' Jesus had said: 'Thy kingdom come' (Lk 11:2). Since Matthew's Jewish readers could misinterpret this as calling for a political messianic kingdom Matthew adds the explanatory words: 'Thy will be done on earth as it is in heaven' (Mt 6:10). He could put these words into Jesus' mouth, because this was exactly what Jesus meant when praying for the Father's kingdom. Jesus taught that disputes should be settled by common discussion. Matthew makes Jesus say that people should refer their problems 'to the church' and that they should 'listen to the church', even though that particular expression, 'the church', arose only in the early Christian community (Mt 18:15-17). The risen Jesus ordered the disciples to proclaim his good news to the whole world. But the formula 'baptising them in the name of the Father, the Son and the Holy Spirit' undoubtedly derived from early liturgical practice (Mt 28:19). Though adhering to Jesus' actual words as much as possible Matthew was not afraid occasionally to interpret them to make sure the readers would understand what Jesus had meant.

A further example of this can be found in the question of divorce. Jesus had declared a clear principle which was simple and uncompromising. He rejected divorce (Lk 16:18; Mk 10:11-12). The early Christian community, however, correctly understood that Jesus was not promulgating *a law;* he was stating *a principle.* And principles allow of exceptions. Paul came across cases that required a decision. Of some married couples, one became a Christian, the other not. With the authority he had as an apostle, Paul decided that, if the non-Christian partner desired a divorce, this should be granted (1 Cor 7:12-16). In the Palestinian community for whom Matthew wrote, it had similarly been decided that 'fornication' (whatever they meant by that term) was a just reason for divorce. Matthew could thus make Jesus say: 'The man who divorces his wife, *except in the case of fornication,* and marries another, is guilty of adultery' (Mt 5:32; 19:9). Although Matthew here enlarges on Jesus' original words, he could do so because Jesus himself had given this power of interpretation to his disciples: 'Whatever you bind on earth shall be bound in heaven; whatever you loose on earth shall be loosed in heaven' (Mt 18:18).[65]

These examples, which have all been taken from Matthew's gospel, could be paralleled by illustrations taken from the other gospels. The gospels deserve to be treated as faithful and historical documents. But they should not be interpreted in a naive and simplistic fashion. The *gospels possess unusual features, due to their particular nature and the cultural expression of the time.* In some narration we find traces of *midrash.* The gospels focus on substance rather than detail. They have a pastoral and theological purpose and are not concerned with historical precision over incidentals. But these traits, on inspection, make them all the more genuine and reliable as faithful records of what Jesus said and did.

9
who saw JESUS saw GOD

Jesus' divinity is by far the most difficult part of the gospel message. Thinking or talking about God is difficult enough in itself; our human thoughts and words are so inadequate to express his being accurately. Speaking about God becoming man is more difficult, if not almost impossible. It is here more than anywhere else that 'the transcendent' and 'history' seem to meet in a most unlikely conjunction.

Did Jesus actually claim he was God? It is a question worth asking because critics often assert that Jesus himself never made such a claim. It was the Christians of later generations who deified him, they say. Sometimes it is even stated that Jesus was only 'made God' at the Council of Nicaea in AD 325. The blame is put on the Emperor Constantine, a man who was 'politically a superb manager of people, but almost certainly theologically illiterate'.[66]

It is true that Jesus Christ never said in so many words: 'I am God.' It is also true that it was only at the Council of Nicaea that the Church coined the phrases of our present creed: 'Jesus Christ, God from God, light from light, only begotten Son, before all ages begotten from the Father, who for our salvation became man.' It took many centuries before our present-day terminology of Jesus' divinity had been worked out. But this was a question of *words,* of finding the best way of *expressing* the Church's belief.

The New Testament writings make abundantly clear that the first century Christians already possessed a very strong and outspoken belief in the doctrine of the Incarnation. A few examples will serve to illustrate this:

Quoting an old Christian hymn, Paul could say: 'Though Jesus Christ was in the form of God, he did not count equality with God as a thing to be grasped, but emptied himself, taking the form of a servant' (Phil 2:6-7).

The prologue of John's gospel states:

In the beginning was the Word and the Word was with God, and the Word was God ... And the Word became flesh and lived among us ... No one has ever seen God; the only begotten Son, who is in the bosom of the Father, he has made him known (Jn 1:1, 14, 18).

And Paul's letter to Titus speaks of the 'appearance of the glory of our great God and Saviour Christ Jesus' (Tit 2:13).

Such texts, though using different terms, express the belief of Christians *in the first century* that Jesus was God living among us, that in him somehow God had taken a human form. The doctrine, the beliefs were there; the problem was how to express it properly.

To appreciate the problem, imagine declaring: 'John Smith is God.' People would burst out laughing. The incongruity is too obvious. It puts a person with a weak human body, a limited human mind and a brief human life on a par with the all powerful, immortal, infinite and eternal God.

gloomy night embrac'd the place
  where the noble infant lay.
the BABE look't up and shew'd his face;
in spite of darkness, it was day.

        it was thy day, sweet!
        and did rise
        not from the East,
        but from thine eyes.

                    RICHARD CRASHAW
                        1613 - 1649

This was the difficulty faced by the early Christians. 'Jesus is God', so glibly trotted out by Christians today, is in reality an astonishing idea. It no longer shocks us only because we have heard it repeated so often, and it only makes sense to us because we have given it a specific interpretation. With 'Jesus is God' we mean that in the historical person Jesus Christ (who was a real human being like you and me) God himself (the one, infinite creator) lived among us.

To express this almost inexpressible doctrine theologians and Church councils added further terminology. Since the Creator and the creature must remain distinct, they stated that we should distinguish in Jesus *two natures:* a divine and a human one. To bring out, however, that the human Jesus himself represented God fully, they speak of their being only *one person* in Jesus, who is both human and divine.

While respecting such traditional terminology we should remember that the meaning of the term 'person' in this context is different from what we today mean by 'a person'. What matters is our belief that Jesus Christ, who was truly human like us, and therefore a 'human person' like us in today's language, was at the same time the reality of God's presence among us.[67]

What did Jesus say about himself? It is clear from a study of the sources that Jesus did not apply to himself the *titles* he would soon be known by among his followers: such as Son of David, Messiah, Saviour, Redeemer, Son of God and Lord. At times he called himself 'the Son of Man', and it is interesting to observe that the early Christians were aware of the special status enjoyed by this title. Although it occurs fifty-one times in the gospels it is always reported in texts where Jesus speaks about himself. It is never used in statements about him by others; nor in prayers addressed to him; nor in formulations of the Creed. It occurs exclusively on the lips of Jesus himself.[68] What did he mean by it?

Volumes have been written on this. They show that in Jesus' time people were speculating about the messianic figure prophesied in Daniel 7:13-14. These verses concern a mysterious Son of Man.

> Behold there came someone like a Son of Man on the clouds of heaven. He came to the Ancient of Days and was presented before him. To him was given dominion and glory and kingdom, so that all peoples, nations and languages should serve him. His dominion will be an everlasting dominion, which shall not pass away.

This 'Son of Man' was expected to reveal himself on the day of God's judgement. He would overthrow evil kings and rulers. He would sit down on a throne of glory and hold judgement. He would prove to be a source of hope for all those who were troubled and a defender of the righteous and holy. All the world was to fall down before him. The righteous and the elect would share a happy life with him.[69]

Jesus' self-image

Jesus applied this image of the Son of Man to himself, enlarging it and giving it at the same time a more specific meaning. Yes, he will come to hold judgement (Lk 21:36). His appearance will be as sudden as a flash of lightning across the sky (Mt 24:27). He will ride in on the clouds, manifesting great power and glory, and sending out his angels to gather God's chosen people from the ends of the world (Mk 13:26-27). He will sit down on the throne at

God's right hand (Lk 22:69). But he will only do this after having proved himself to be the 'suffering servant' announced in Isaiah. He came 'not to be served, but to serve, namely to give his life as a ransom for many' (Mk 10:45; Is 53:10-11). He was to 'pour out his blood for many for the forgiveness of sins' (Mt 26:28; Is 53 *passim*). Jesus would bring God's definitive judgement, but only after offering the gift of redemption.[70]

Jesus' contemporaries knew: Only God is the judge, only God can save. But Jesus consistently claimed a role in both functions. Jesus often speaks not just as a prophet, on behalf of God. He speaks with his own authority, *as if he were God*. Consider, for instance, the six antitheses which Matthew brought together in a dramatic sequence (Mt 5:21-48). Six times Jesus contrasts his own commandments with laws promulgated by God in the Old Testament:

> You have heard how it was said to our fathers, 'You may not kill.' But I say to you . . . .

> You have heard how it was said, 'You may not commit adultery.' But I say to you . . . .

> It has also been said, 'Anyone who divorces his wife must give her a writ of dismissal.' But I say this to you . . . .

Jesus perfected and completed the Old Testament laws (Mt 5:17-19). He did so with an enormous sense of authority. He spoke with an emphatic 'I tell you' that was unique.[71] Jesus coined the phrase 'Amen I say to you,' which is without any parallel in the whole of Jewish literature and the rest of the New Testament.[72] It occurs fifty-nine times in the Gospels. Its usage is strictly confined to the words of Jesus himself. It expresses more than just conviction; it makes Jesus' statements equivalent to divine oracles.[73] People realised this. 'The crowds were astonished at his teaching for he taught them as one who had authority, and not as their scribes' (Mt 7:28-29).

The Temple in Jerusalem was for the Jews the holiest object on earth. Any form of desecration or blasphemy against it was punishable with death. But Jesus claimed that he was greater than the Temple (Mt 12:5-6). Through his resurrection he would build a new temple of greater value (Mk 14:58). He would found a community of believers that would be indestructible (Mt 16:18). From now on people could worship the Father anywhere, as long as they would do so in spirit and in truth (Jn 4:20-24). The holiness of the Temple derived from God himself. How could anyone except God abolish its status?

Everyone knew that God alone could give life. 'I alone am God. No other God exists. It is I who kill and I who give life, I cause disease and I can heal. No one can oppose what I do' (Dt 32:39). But Jesus heals in his own name; with authority. To the leper he says: 'I will it; be clean' (Mk 1:41). He tells the paralytic: 'I say to you, get up, take up your bed and go home' (Mk 2:11). Taking the hand of a child who had died, he ordered her: 'Little girl, I say to you, get up' (Mk 5:41). Jesus cured an epileptic by driving out the demon that caused the disease:[74] 'You dumb and deaf spirit, I command you, come out of him and never enter this person again' (Mk 9:25). John's gospel concludes in so many words: 'As the Father raises the dead and gives them life, so also the Son gives life to whom he will' (Jn 5:21).

When Jesus forgave a man's sins, the bystanders were scandalized. 'Who can forgive sins but God alone?' Jesus performed a miracle 'that you may know that the Son of Man has authority on earth to forgive sins' (Mk 2:6-10).

Again, the Jews knew that only almighty God had control over the sea. 'Who kept the sea within closed doors . . .? It was I who marked the bounds it is not to cross, who has set it bars and doors. I said, "So far you shall come, and no further! Here shall your proud ways be halted!" (Job 38:8-11).' But Jesus walked on the water (Mt 14:25). And when there was a storm, he ordered the wind to die down and the sea to be still. Small wonder that those who witnessed it were overcome with awe. 'Who can this be that even the wind and the sea obey him?' (Mk 4:39-41).

Jesus and the Father

It will be difficult, from a historical point of view, to establish each and every one of these instances beyond doubt. Later generations may have exaggerated events in passing them on, or may have given new interpretations. The meaning of an event may have been highlighted by making Jesus say explicitly what was implied in the happening itself. This is particularly the case in St John's gospel.[75] But there can be no doubt about the fact that Jesus, both through his words and his deeds, made extraordinary and unprecedented claims.

Think carefully about the meaning of these words: 'Whoever receives me, receives not me but him who sent me' (Mk 9:37). 'Every person who acknowledges me before people, I also will acknowledge before my Father who is in heaven' (Mt 10:32). 'He who loves father or mother more than me is not worthy of me' (Mt 10:37). At the last judgement people will be rewarded or punished according to the love they showed him. 'As you did to one of the least of my brethren, you did it to me' (Mt 25:40-45). Matthew sums it all up at the end of his gospel: 'All authority in heaven and on earth; says Jesus, 'has been given to me' (Mt 28:18).

Notice how Jesus says that his authority had been *given* to him. He never denies complete dependence on God, whom he called his Father. On account of that dependence he could say: 'The Father is greater than I' (Jn 14:28). But he claimed at the same time an exclusive relationship to the Father, a relationship going much beyond that existing between God and a prophet. 'All things have been handed over to me by my Father. No one knows the Son except the Father, and no one knows the Father except the Son and anyone to whom the Son chooses to reveal him' (Mt 11:27). We can be reasonably certain Jesus really spoke these words.[76] They express the essence of his own personality as revealing God. The same is expressed in John's gospel by the words: 'Whoever sees me, sees the Father' (Jn 14:9).[77]

This then is what Jesus claimed and what Christians believe: that in Jesus God himself appeared among us. In what Jesus did, people could see God act. In Jesus' words they could hear the Father speak. Like the resurrection which we discussed earlier, the whole of Jesus' life has the double quality of being rooted in history and transcending history at the same time. It could be observed with human eyes, yet required faith to respond to its divine dimension. Historians can do no more than record the extraordinary claims Jesus made; believers will see these claims confirmed by the new awareness of God they offer.

Whatever the measure of our response, it is worth recalling Chesterton's reflections at this point. Great religious leaders, he reminds us, have no pretensions.

'Normally speaking, the greater a man is, the less likely he is to make the very greatest claim.' Only a madman will put himself on a par with God.

> But this is exactly where the argument becomes intensely interesting; because the argument proves too much. For nobody supposes that Jesus of Nazareth was *that* sort of person. No modern critic in his five wits thinks that the preacher of the sermon on the mount was a horrible half-witted imbecile that might be scrawling stars on the walls of a cell. No atheist or blasphemer believes that the author of the parable of the prodigal son was a monster with one mad idea like a cyclops with one eye. Upon any possible historical criticism, he must be put higher in the scale of human beings than that. Yet by all analogy we have really to put him there or else in the highest place of all.'[78]

There have been, indeed, people who claimed to be God, in one way or other. No one however has done so in the way Jesus did, with his disarming integrity, nor with such lasting success.

10

'I will be with you till the end of time'

More than twenty years ago I spent two months walking the length and breadth of Palestine. It was an exciting time. I remember a discussion I had in Capernaum, among the ruins of the ancient synagogue. It was the very place where John stages Jesus' eucharistic sermon. 'Who eats my flesh and drinks my blood will never die' (Jn 6:54-58). I had joined a Hungarian student for the day. He scowled at my belief.

'Suppose you were Almighty God,' he said to me. 'And suppose that in the goodness of your heart you had decided to make yourself known to mankind. What good would it do to come down on earth at a particular time in one specific country? You would meet only a small group of people. You would still be as far as ever from those born elsewhere or centuries later. What good is Jesus Christ to me, even if he was God incarnate? For me he is just a figure from the past. If God wants to speak to me he should do so here and now.'

My friend had a point. And without realising it, he had put his finger on the historians' blind spot. Whoever studies Jesus Christ solely from the limited angle of secular history is bound to end up with nothing but bits and pieces belonging to a figure of the past. Christians believe that the historical evidence makes sense only if we see it as part of a comprehensive, *present* reality. The Jesus who revealed God in his historical life remains with us now as a tangible presence. Jesus promised Nathanael: 'You will see a ladder between heaven and earth with angels climbing up and down' (Jn 1:51). What use is such a ladder to us if *we* cannot see it? What use are Jesus' miracles in Galilee if he performs no signs for us *in London?*

> But (when so sad thou canst not sadder),
> Cry—and upon thy so sore loss
> Shall shine the traffic of Jacob's ladder
> Pitched between Heaven and Charing Cross.
>
> Yea, in the night, my Soul, my daughter,
> Cry—clinging heaven by the hems;
> And lo, Christ walking on the water,
> Not of Gennesareth, but Thames!
> > Francis Thompson *In No Strange Land* [79]

When we discussed the resurrection we saw that it means Jesus' continuing presence as an active, spiritual force. He is alive and stays with us, completing on a spiritual plane what he had begun in his historical life. Jesus' farewell discourse in John's gospel announces this presence clearly and emphatically.

> *'I will reveal myself to you'* (see Jn 14:21). The context makes clear that Jesus is speaking to every one of his disciples, including those of later generations. The only condition he makes is that to see him you must put into practice Jesus' commandments of love.

> *'My Father and I shall come and make our home in you'* (see Jn 14:23).

> *'The world will not see me but you will see me'* (Jn 14:19).

'I shall be in you and you shall be in me' (Jn 14:20).

These words of Jesus express as clearly as it can be said that he left a promise to remain with every one of his disciples in a tangible form. He did not say he would appear to them as a ghost with a phantom body. On the other hand, his presence would not be a mere invisible shadow. As I have explained in *Experiencing Jesus,* [80] Jesus' teaching can have no other meaning than a promise of his visible presence. The disciple will be aware of what Jesus does for him or her. The disciple will see him, hear him, feel Jesus' support and enjoy his encouragement. What is more: Jesus' own Spirit will operate in us. He will teach us, console us, strengthen us and give Jesus' vision fresh, dynamic applications in our life. [81]

It is in this way that Jesus Christ both entered history and transcended history. It is the historical and yet transcendent Jesus who, we believe, meets each person today and who offers salvation. Jesus' word invites us to accept the love of his Father. Jesus washes us clean in baptism so that we are born anew as God's adopted children. Jesus offers sacrifice on our behalf whenever we 'break the bread and drink the wine' in his memory. He comes to us as the spiritual bread that makes us live forever. Jesus forgives our sins when the priest, in his name, speaks the words of absolution. It is the sacramental presence of Jesus that gives life to his people, the Church.

Then there is the social dimension of Christ. Jesus had said he would be visible in his followers, 'Who receives you, receives me' (Mt 10:40). 'Who hears you, hears me' (Lk 10:16). Wherever Jesus' followers are involved in his work, filled by his Spirit of love and continuing his life-giving service, Jesus will be seen in them. The fourth century Augustine of Hippo could have been speaking of Father

Damian among the lepers, Maximilian Kolbe in Auschwitz or Mother Teresa in Calcutta when he said:

> Pay attention to the Church, I tell you. Pay attention to whom you *can* see ... The inhabitants of Palestine who were open to faith could learn from Mary about his birth, his passion, resurrection and ascension. The words and deeds of Jesus were accessible to them. They could observe those divine actions from nearby. But you have not seen those things and therefore, you say, you don't believe. Look then at the Church. Fix your eyes and mind on what you *can* see today, on what is not reported to you as the past nor foretold as the future; on what is presented as topical now.[82]

Christians often fail to live up to their ideals. But in those who do, Christ's lasting presence can be seen with unmistakable clarity. No single person in the history of mankind has inspired so much dedication and heroism in so many millions of followers as Christ has. Every Christian has recognised this manifestation of Christ: in the faith of family and friends, in the zeal of spiritual leaders, in the worship of the parish community, in the love of those who are truly 'Christian'.

Christ *is* powerfully present today, but we may not be aware of his action because it is not the kind of thing published in the news. Modern society, in fact, treats religious experience as a taboo. The media avoid touching on it; and if they do, they will cushion their report with sarcasm or scepticism. Individuals do not easily admit to religious experiences. They are afraid others will consider them crazy, as research has proved.[83] The result is a narrowing of our range of observation. To see Christ at work we must either believe and sense his closeness in our

own life or learn from friends who share their experiences
with us.

Occasionally Christ's presence breaks through in
publications and films. In *The Cross and the Switchblade* we
can read the true story of how a New York preacher took
Jesus' saving power right into the heart of that city's hell-
holes. It describes how young people in the clutches of
unemployment, crime, prostitution and drug addiction
found a new life in Christ. In one dramatic scene the
minister narrates how he spoke to a gang and invited their
leaders to step forward. 'I want you to kneel down right
here on the street and ask the Holy Spirit to come into your
lives so that you will become new people. ''New creatures
in Christ'' is what the Bible says: this can happen to you
too.' After some hesitation the miracle took place.

> Before my astonished eyes, these two leaders of one
> of the most feared fighting gangs in all of New York
> slowly dropped to their knees. Their War Lords
> followed their lead. They took their hats off and held
> them respectfully in front of them. Two of the boys
> had been smoking. Each took his cigarette out of his
> mouth and flipped it away, where it lay smoldering
> in the gutter while I said a very short prayer.[84]

Father Walter Ciszek, an American Jesuit, was
captured by the Russian army during World War II and
was convicted of being a 'Vatican spy'. He spent twenty-
three agonizing years in Soviet prisons and the labour
camps of Siberia. In his book, *He Leadeth Me,* he tells of
the endless interrogations, tortures and, especially, inner
despair he endured for years on end; till he was suddenly
transformed by a new awareness of Christ that gave him
the strength to carry on. He remembered Jesus' agony in
the Garden of Gethsemane. He understood how Jesus' plea

one of the crowd went up,
and knelt before the paten and the cup,
received the LORD, returned in peace and prayed
close to my side; then in my heart I said:

'o CHRIST, in this man's life —
this stranger who is thine — in all his strife,
all his felicity, his good and ill,
in the assaulted stronghold of his will,

'I do confess thee here,
alive within this life; I know thee near
within this lonely conscience, closed away
within this brother's solitary day.

'Christ in his unknown heart,
his intellect unknown — this love, this art,
this battle and this peace, this destiny
that I shall never know, look upon me!

'Christ in his numbered breath,
Christ in his beating heart and in his death,
Christ in his mystery! from that secret place
and from that separate dwelling, give me grace.'

ALICE MEYNELL
1847 - 1922

for help and Jesus' surrender to his Father's will underpinned his own desperate prayer.

> What a wonderful treasure and source of strength and consolation our Lord's agony in the garden became for me from that moment on. I saw clearly exactly what I must do. I can only call it a conversion experience, and I can only tell you frankly that my life was changed from that moment on. If my days of despair had been days of total blackness, then this was an experience of blinding light. I knew immediately what I must do, what I would do, and somehow I knew that I could do it. I knew that I must abandon myself entirely to the will of the Father. And I did it.[85]

I cite these examples because they illustrate so vividly that Christ is alive today, as much as he was alive 2000 years ago. He is present in the home and the workshop, in the church and the swimming pool, in hospitals and market places; in fact, wherever people carry him in their hearts and make him present. He is as much at home in the igloo of the Eskimo as the mud hut of a Kenyan Masai. He inspires people in ministerial offices in Rio de Janeiro no less than in the concentration camps of Vietnam. He can be present in this way because by his life-giving resurrection he transcends history.

This makes the Incarnation eminently believable. The objection of my Hungarian friend at Capernaum is decisively answered by it. 'Whoever eats my flesh and drinks my blood lives in me, and I live in him' (Jn 6:56). God's revelation in Jesus Christ was not a short-lived venture in an isolated spot centuries ago. Like any real happening in our world it needed such a precise historical insertion in time and place. But from this historical landing-point ripples of his presence and waves of his power have widened in ever wider circles to span the totality of human space.

John, in exile on the island of Patmos, encountered his Master in a vision of light. Christ's words to him are addressed to each one of us:

Don't be afraid!
I was dead, but now I live for ever and ever.
I have authority over death
    and the world of the dead.
I am the one who has life.
I am the first and the last.

Rev 1:17-18

1. Thomas Dekker (1570-1641); Joseph Addison (1672-1719); Albert Camus (1913-1960).
2. IAN WILSON, *The Shroud of Turin,* Doubleday, New York 1979.
3. S. WALKER and S. BURNETT, *The Image of Augustus,* British Museum Publication, London 1981.
4. D. THOMAS, *The Face of Christ,* Hamlyn, London 1979.
5. W. A. BEARDSLEY, 'Truth in the Study of Religion', in *Truth, Myth and Symbol,* ed. T. J. J. ALTIZER, Prentice-Hall, Englewood Cliffs 1962, pp.61-75.
6. A. LOISY, cf. X. LEON-DUFOUR, *Les évangiles et l'histoire de Jésus,* Du Seuil, Paris 1963, p.81.
7. H. C. KEE and F. W. YOUNG, *Understanding the New Testament,* Prentice-Hall, Englewood Cliffs, Dutch Bosch & Keuning, Baarn 1965, vol 3, p.86.
8. M. BAILLET, J. T. MILIK and R. de VAUX *Discoveries in the Judaean Desert of Jordan,* vol III, Oxford 1962, p.271. See also: J. JEREMIAS, *The Rediscovery of Bethesda,* Louisville 1966.
9. P. J. GEYER, *Itinera Hierosolymita,* Vienna 1898, p.21.
10. Homily on the Paralysed Man II. PC XXXIII 1133.
11. J. KLINGER, 'Bethesda and the universality of the Logos', *St Vladimir's Theological Quarterly* 27 (1983) 169-185.
12. The explanation that an angel touched the water from time to time (Jn 5:3b-4) is a gloss added by a copyist. It is not found in the most ancient manuscripts.
13. B. SCHWANK, 'Ortskenntnisse im Vierten Evangelium', *Erbe und Auftrag* 57 (1981) 427-442.
14. J. MARSH, *St John,* Penguin 1968, p.249.
15. E. H. CARR. *What is History? Reflections on the theory of history and the role of the historian,* Penguin 1985, p.29.
16. J. KREMER, *Das aelteste Zeugnis von der Auferstehung Christi* Stuttgart 1970, p.29-30.
17. H. SCHLIER, *Die Zeit der Kirche,* Freiburg 1956, p.230.
18. B. GERHARDSON, *Memory and Manuscript,* Uppsala 1961, p.297.
19. J. MANEK, 'The Apostle Paul and the empty Tomb' *Novum Testamentum* 2 (1957) 276-280.

20. J. JEREMIAS, *Heiligen Graeber in Jesu Umwelt,* Goettingen 1958.

21. J. DELORME, 'Résurrection et Tombeau de Jésus', in *La Resurrection du Christ et l'Exégèse Moderne,* ed. P. DE SURGY, Paris 1969, p.105-151. It was natural that this record would be amplified from other sources in Mt 27:57—28,8; Lk 28:1-15.

22. Mt 16:21; 17:23; 20:19; 27:64; Lk 9:22; 13:32; 18:33; 24:7,21,46; Acts 10:40; 1 Cor 15:4.

23. Mt 26:61; Mk 8:31; 9:31; 10:34; 13:2; 14:58; 15:29; Jn 2:19,20. Once the expression 'after three days and three nights' is used under influence of the Jonah story (Mt 12:40).

24. Fr von CAMPENHAUSEN, *Der Ablauf der Osterereignisse und der Leere Grab,* Heidelberg 1958, p.11-12.

25. W. RORDORF, *Sunday. The History of the Day of Rest and Worship in the earliest centuries of the Christian Church,* London 1968, pp.229-236.

26. D. HUME, *Essay concerning human understanding;* in A. DULLES, *Apologetics and the biblical Christ,* London 1962, p.62.

27. In *De Bazuin,* 17 April 1981, pp.51-55; English translation my own.

28. E. BENZ, *Paulus als Visionaer,* Wiesbaden 1952.

29. J. WIJNGAARDS, 'Assessing Spiritual Experiences', *The Clergy Review* 67 (1982), pp. 253-260.

30. *Summa Theologica* III q 55 a2. ad 1 (oculata fide).

31. I have described this experience more fully and documented it with many illustrations in *Experiencing Jesus,* Ave Maria Press, Notre Dame 1983.

32. Editorial in *Life,* 1956; Time, Inc. See *Encyclopedia of Religious Quotations,* ed. F. S. MEAD, London 1965, p.379.

33. N. BREUNING, 'Death and Resurrection in the Christian message', *Concilium* 4 (1968), pp.5-13.

34. T. VAN DER STAP, 'Waar ontmoet ik de Verrijzenis?', *Streven* 20 (1967), pp.647-650.

35. J. RATZINGER, *Einfuehrung in das Christentum,* Munich 1969, p.249.

36. J. RATZINGER, ibid. pp.254-255.
37. PAUL VI, 'Easter Message', *Osservatore Romano*, 13 April 1972.
38. W. KUNNETH, *The Theology of the Resurrection*, London 1965, pp.78-80.
39. R. BULTMANN, *Jesus*, Siebenstern 1926, p.145.
40. Lk 9:21-22; 9:43-45; 13:33-35; 18:31-34; 20:13-18; 22:14-22; 22:37;
41. CICERO, *De Oratore II* 62.
42. THUCYDIDES, *History of the Peloponnesian War I*, 22.1.
43. LUCIAN, *On History Writing*, ch. 47.
44. FLAVIUS JOSEPHUS, *Contra Apionem* I, par.9.
45. A. W. MOSLEY, 'Historical Reporting in the Ancient World', *New Testament Studies* 12 (1965), pp.10-26.
46. L. ALEXANDER, 'Luke's preface in the Context of Greek preface-writing', *Novum Testamentum* 28 (1986), pp.48-74.
47. W. MEEKS, 'The Social Context of Pauline Theology', *Interpretation* 36 (1982), p.270.
48. J. SOIRON, *Die Bergpredigt*, Freiburg 1941, p.139.
49. K. BORNHAUSER, *Die Bergpredigt*, Guetersloh 1923, p.11.
50. *Mishna Awot* 5:2,8.
51. See for example C. F. BURNEY, *The poetry of our Lord*, Oxford 1925; L. DE GRANDMAISON, *Jesus Christ*, Paris 1929, vol.I.
52. C. C. TORREY even translated the Gospels back into Aramaic. *The Four Gospels*, London 1933.
53. W. F. ALBRIGHT, *The Archeology of Palestine*, Penguin, p.248.
54. Mk 3:14; 6:6-13; Mt 9:35-10:42; Lk 6:13; 9:1-6; 10:1-20.
55. H. SCHUERMANN, 'Die voroesterlichen Anfaenge der Logientradition', in *Der historische Jesus und der kerugmatische Christus* ed. H. RISTOW and K. MATTHIAE, Berlin 1962, pp.342-270.
56. H. RIESENFELD, *The Gospel Tradition and its Beginnings*, London 1957.

57. We can see this by comparing the official list in 1 Chron 3:10-16 with Mt 1:7-11.

58. 'David' is composed of three consonants in Hebrew: *daleth* (value:4), *waw* (value:6), *daleth* (value:4). Together, value:14.

59. P. F. HERSHON, *A Talmudic Miscellany,* London 1880 (ad Gen 22:1).

60. Lev. R.Emor 29,9.

61. A. COHEN, *Everyman's Talmud,* London 1961, p.56.

62. Sanhedrin 89, col.2.

63. J. WIJNGAARDS, 'The Episode of the Magi and Christian Kerygma', *Indian Journal of Theology* 16 (1967), pp.30-41; see also M. M. BOURKE, 'The Literary Genus of Matthew 1-2', *Catholic Biblical Quarterly* 22 (1960), pp.160-175.

64. J. WIJNGAARDS, 'Ancient Prophets on My Mountain', in *Inheriting the Master's Cloak,* Notre Dame 1985, pp.83-88.

65. J. WIJNGAARDS, 'Do Jesus' Words on Divorce Admit of No Exception?' *Jeevadhara* 4 (1975), pp.399-411.

66. J. WILSON, *Jesus: The Evidence,* London 1984, pp.140-142.

67. K. RAHNER, 'God's Oneness and Trinity', *Schriften zur Theologie,* vol XIII,pp.129-147.

68. Jn 12:34 is not a real exception. The crowd uses the expression but only because they quote Jesus' own words.

69. Similitudes of Ethiopian Enoch; Sibylline Oracles; IV Esra; Justin, in *Dialogues;* rabbinic literature. H. L. STRACK— P. BILLERBECK, *Kommentar zum Neuen Testament aus Talmud und Midrasch,* Vol I, Munich 1922, pp.486,956-958.

70. J. JEREMIAS, *New Testament Theology,* London 1971, pp.257-299.

71. J. JEREMIAS, ibid, pp. 251-253.

72. J. JEREMIAS, *Abba. Studien zur neutestamentlichen Theologie und Zeitgeschichte,* Goettingen 1966, pp.148-151.

73. T. W. MANSON, *The Teaching of Jesus,* Cambridge 1931, p.207.

74. In Jesus' day it was commonly held that certain diseases were caused by demons whom God allowed to afflict a human person. In many cases the exorcisms are parallel to healings.

75. I give many examples in my commentary on John. See: J. WIJNGAARDS, *The Gospel of John and his Letters,* Michael Glazier, Wilmington 1986.

76. J. JEREMIAS, *Abba,* etc. op.cit., pp.47-54.

77. J. WIJNGAARDS, *The Gospel of John,* op.cit., pp.131-144.

78. G. K. CHESTERTON, *The Everlasting Man,* New York 1925, p.201.

79. F. THOMPSON, 'In No Strange Land'; from *The Divine Office,* vol.III, Collins, London 1974, p.803*.

80. J. WIJNGAARDS, *Experiencing Jesus,* op.cit., pp.3-18.

81. J. WIJNGAARDS, *The Gospel of John,* op.cit., pp.184-194.

82. AUGUSTINE, 'De fide rerum quae non videntur', IV,7; in *Migne Latinum* vol.XL, p.76.

83. See D. HAY, *Exploring Inner Space,* Penguin 1982.

84. D. WILKERSON, *The Cross and the Switchblade,* Lakeland Paperback 1967, p.59.

85. W. J. CISZEK, *He Leadeth Me,* Doubleday 1975, p.87.